Rob Silverstone has worked for many years as a chef, including in the Michelin star kitchen of Michel Guérard. He is very keen on healthy eating and has lectured in food & nutrition at two universities. He has run his own restaurants, 'The Cook & Fiddle' under the Arches on Brighton beach, and 'Le Moulin de Mule' in Rouen. The gothic architecture of old Rouen inspired an interest in black and white photography, and exhibitions have followed at Brighton Museum and Le Musée Maritime on the Seine.

Also by Rob Silverstone

A Mule in Rouen – A Discovery of Upper Normandy
ISBN 978-1-84386-997-9

'The secrets of Normandy countryside discovered by bike, and the tale of a Brighton chef setting up shop in France.'

Read more adventures of the Mule, including another chapter on Brighton.

"If you enjoyed Peter Mayles' 'A Year in Provence' you're bound to like this similar account of Rob Silverstone's experience in Normandy."

The Brighton Argus

"An excellent read. Silverstone's engaging account of setting up a restaurant in Normandy is a reminder that not all plans run smoothly. What he lacks in luck as an entrepreneur he certainly makes up for as a writer."

Everything France

"An engaging diary-cum-travel log written in a pleasing, informal style. Travelling largely by bicycle through Normandy, Silverstone can make a bar redolent of Edith Piaf with a short, evocative turn of phrase. He is at his best when reading Flaubert's Madame Bovary and drawing perceptive comparisons with what he sees around him."

The Sussex Express

A Mule In Brighton – A Taste of the Downs
ISBN: 978-184386-310-6

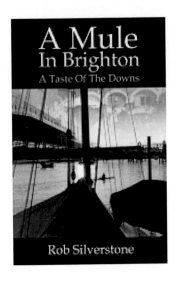

"Some of the delights to be found in this terrific book. It has a stroll down memory lane, a view of contemporary Brighton, a visit to heritage sites, a photographic gallery and even some terrific recipes. It is a book which will be enjoyed by residents and visitors to the city alike. Presented in an easy going and accessible style it offers something for everyone."

www.mybrightonandhove.org.uk

Rob Silverstone

A Mule Across the Water

Real Food in Sussex and Normandy

Vanguard Press

A CIP catalogue record for this title is
available from the British Library.

ISBN 978 1 84386 759 3

Vanguard Press is an imprint of
Pegasus Elliot MacKenzie Publishers Ltd.
www.pegasuspublishers.com

Permission has been obtained to use the Scalands Farm and
Hammerpot Brewery logos respectively.

Permission has been obtained from the authors of the Sussex map. The Avenue
Verte map comes from a free website which is acknowledged below. The Normandy
map already appears in 'A Mule in Rouen' – permission was obtained in 2004.

First Published in 2014

Vanguard Press
Sheraton House Castle Park
Cambridge England

Printed & Bound in Great Britain

To Mum and Grandma Fish – two great cooks

Acknowledgements

To all the local chefs and producers who contributed such appetising recipes.

To Judy Moore, author of an invaluable book on local food, *Sampling Sussex,* published by S.B. Publications, 1996.

Contents

Chapter 1

A Mule Across the Water

The best ever comedy night in Brighton was Thursday in a packed, low-ceilinged bar above the Aquarium. The 'Crocodile Club' always opened with a slot for local talent, the audience waiting to pounce and destroy at the slightest scent of weakness. Master of Ceremonies Terry Garogan had a canny card up his sleeve. Whenever unable to conjure laughs from the latest issue of the 'Leader', the boisterous crowd at the back of the bar baying for his baldy head, he would unleash a booming Tom Jones number that left the hecklers for dead. That old club was not much more than a scout hut billowing with smoke. You always emerged into the outside world, vocal chords smouldering like Marlene Dietrich. Then off for a night at the Zap Club where the dense, dark, nicotine cloud propped up the ancient arches from the pounding roll of traffic.

Last Thursday I had the strange experience of watching Jim's band play above a pub in a totally smokeless room. I kept looking over my shoulder for a familiar presence gone missing. There was something sterile about the place, cold and not quite Brighton. An inordinate amount of bouncers patrolled up and down, bull neck, pin point eyes, skull rippling with muscles. Ear piece buzzing with electric noise, stirring the sleeping demons. The chief bouncer hit the lights as the last chords still resounded, announcing in security speak, 'Event over, thank you very much, now toddle off to bed.' Clothes clean, mind clear, but feel good factor dead.

A similar rather sanitised experience at a pub on Hanover hill. A wine tasting presided over by a wan priest when the occasion demanded Friar Tuck. Notes scribbled down in silence, samples chomped awkwardly then spouted into a spittoon. A night out at the dentist. Not a sniff of Sussex wine the entire evening, a grave omission in my book having recently discovered the vineyard at Breaky Bottom. Cycled off to Rodmell on the River Ouse, with a blacksmith's forge where a garage once stood. The petrol pump attendant's hut now bursting with geraniums. Climbed the hill past Northease Farm, and there in a hollow of The Downs, the vineyard shone in the early morning sun. A solid stone farmhouse, softened by willows, and inside the proprietor busy preparing a breakfast of porridge and kippers. His family descends from the Normandy village of Petit Torcy, where sloping thatched cottages are garlanded with flowers, and happy cows churn the grass into rounds of butter and Camembert.

A gathering of friends and cognoscenti helped bottle the wine in a dark barn pierced by a single shaft of light. Pipes rigged, valves attached and wine coursing into bottles through something resembling a milking machine. Peter Hall must have been considered mad when he first planted vines over thirty years ago, and there is an eccentric air about the place. A Red Indian wigwam inside the farm gates, and a woman moulding lemon halves and turning them into breasts. Visions of lemon breasts bobbling along the vines during a happy pagan harvest. Grapes crushed beneath dancing feet, nooky under the rafters, a bacchanalian feast.

Returned to Rodmell for an excellent veggie lasagna at 'The Abergavenny Arms', a real pub with a big hearth and bustling conversation. There's a lovely little church at the end of the village, with an inscription above the door, 'In the beginning god laughed.' In 1864 an impressive stained glass window was donated by 'Benjamin Godfrey Windus of Tottenham, Middlesex.' Benjamin would have needed that godly sense of humour if alive in Tottenham these past twenty years; following the Spurs has been a biblical tale of tribulation. Until that is, the renaissance in fortunes inspired by Harry 'My dog files my tax returns' Redknapp. Silverware finally within our grasp; crack open the Breaky Bottom.

***

All regular arrivals at Dieppe head for a familiar eatery on Quai Henri IV, napkins flourished beside a sea of bobbing masts. For years I favoured the 'Restaurant du Port'; menu set in stone, solid Norman clientele and the novelty of being served by Edith Piaf's little sister. Until that is, the 'Le Pollet' district underwent something of a gastronomic renaissance. 'Café Jehan Ango' is filled to the gunnels with unusual memorabilia. A washing tub in the corner, with mangle and giant tongs, ancient pressure cookers on the window sills and Mohammed Ali posters on the walls. Old dappled rum bottles line the bar infused with ginger, kiwi and passion fruit. The telephone rings with a bygone chime, the operator arching an eyebrow at a sultry, whispered conversation.

On the '14 euro formule' there is prawn and mussel salad with loads of parsley and homemade mayonnaise; a succulent wing of skate slipping easily off the bone; and a sharp creamy Roquefort to accompany the local cheese. There is also a huge à la carte menu on the wall, old traditional bone breakers like Tripes and Sauerkraut, and novelties such as cassoulet of snails with a cep and morel sauce. Two splendid waitresses maintain a relay of plates above the crowd, the chef emerging at intervals to replenish his litre carafe of red wine. Barrel belly bound in a solid mauve apron, hefty jowls and an emphatic walrus moustache.

On the return trip I plumped for monkfish livers, having never tried this delicacy before, known by gourmets as 'woodcock of the sea.' Intensely fishy, clean and fresh. Made for the boat, and an early evening 'apéro' at the bar 'Mieux Ici Qu'en Face.' Always a toothy welcome and an unparalleled view of the port as it subsides into a soothing twilight blue. The road to the ferry is lined by cliffs which were once home to fishing folk. The photographer Georges Marchand captured pictures of grubby faces, proudly proprietorial in front of their caves. He invented the 'carte postale', portraying scenes of ordinary Dieppe life. Heavily skirted fishwives collecting shellfish on the beach. A restaurant under the colonnade advertising 'Dîner à 2 francs', the chef with wild eyes and floppy white hat, the waiting staff more tranquil.

Another artist who eschewed portraits of the rich was the Impressionist William Sickert, who arrived in Dieppe in 1883 with a letter of introduction to Manet. He specialised in buxom voluptuous Dieppoise, and it is this fascination with 'femmes fatales' which led some to identify him as the real Jack the Ripper. The creative celebrity of Dieppe, then the premier coastal resort, was shot through with non-conformity. Oscar Wilde held court at the 'Café des Tribunaux', his first port of call after release from Reading jail. The father of the artist Jacques Emile Blanche, tended Maupassant as he succumbed to syphilis. A tempestuous mix of art and the flesh that is a far cry from Dieppe today. Nothing more decadent to do after dark than share a lobster at the 'Restaurant du Port' and shuck an oyster for all it's worth.

You can view Sickert among the Impressionists in the Château Musée on the hill. Alongside the birds of Georges Braque, the mesmeric blue of Raoul Dufy, and a striking marine sunset by Charles-Francois Daubigny. My street in Brighton just happens to be named after Daubigny, so there's a daily reminder of the artist, who like Monet, used a houseboat as a floating studio. Not as famous but well worth a visit is 'Les Manuelles', the little artisan workshop on the Rue de la Halle au Blé. 'Les Manuelles' is a play on words, revealing how resident artist Emmanuelle makes every object by hand. I used to frequent this road when it was home to Le

Café de l'Union, once filled with fishing folk, kept in line by an indomitable Madame, who offered hearty lunch and a carafe of wine for nothing more than a fiver. There were also a few rooms upstairs and I imagined them to be wonderfully sparse, mattress filled with horse hair and a cracked china wash bowl. The one time I attempted to book a room, the 'hotel' was full for 'La Fête des Cerfs Volants', and Madame hung up as I struggled with the concept of a 'Festival of flying stags'. I later learnt not to try a literal translation; 'cerf volant' is a kite, and one weekend every September, enthusiasts gather from across the land to fly their kites on the beach. This and the 'Herring Festival' are about the only times that Dieppe attracts a crowd. Our lovely little ferry port that doesn't have a motorway, refugee camp or giant Tesco.

***

Sightings of snow in Brighton are something of a mirage. Draw the curtains at bedtime on a whirlwind of starry flakes, and wake up in the morning to find it all gone. Just a dollop of icing on the postbox receding to grubby red. Until that is, February 2nd 2009 when the snow settled, cars were marooned and the Royal Pavilion emerged as a castle in fairyland. Even the beach glowed brightly in its snug white coat. There were sightings of igloos on Hollingbury golf course, skiers down Ditchling Road, and on The Level the whole of Brighton came out to play. 'Saint Peter's' church lost its sense of sadness, students juggled snowballs and school kids rolled up the belly of a big, big snowman.

The news was full of transport chaos, the ferry dodging icebergs, convoys lost on the A27, the city cut off from the capital. A lovely excuse for the silent army of commuters to pull up the drawbridge and stay in bed. A development on the employment front means that Mister Mule will be joining them three days a week. Rising at an improbable hour, tearing up Trafalgar Street and vaulting the ticket barrier in search of a seat. How long will it be before I assume the grey, faceless insularity of the commuter mass? Straining at the bit as the train pulls into Victoria, the doors stubbornly refusing to part. Then flying across the station concourse, leaving the lame and laggards for dead, diving inside the Tube entrails before emerging flushed at the office. Throughout the day, time ticking towards the nightmare of the return leg, when the entire population of the Seven Dials is sandwiched onto a single train. Ever since the line was opened in 1841, no one has got off at Wivelsfield, yet each night the train grinds to a halt, cogitates for an interminable length of time, then finally ambles on. Three Bridges, Burgess Hill and Hassocks, names plucked out of nowhere, the tally of stops faithfully recounted with a metronomic beat. Stoical, unhurried progress through the cutting, out of the tunnel and then a quiet sense of celebration as the sparkling hills of Brighton take hold. Until that is, the onset of snow, and Thomas the Tank Engine puffs on his pipe and settles for life in the shed.

The pattern of immersion into the Time Tunnel to London was broken by the 'Body on the Line at Balcombe.' A sense of foreboding grew like a darkening sky. Papers snapped at the delay, then consternation at cancellation and finally all aboard the slow boat to Haywards Heath where we were disgorged into a car park. The crowd seethed to and fro, desperate for a sense of certainty. Had war broken out? Was Lenin dead? Would we make the 7.45 kick off at White Hart Lane? Rumour spread of buses laid on by the U.N., succeeded by plans to spend the night in a school gymnasium. As if by magic, a taxi appeared, and a lady asked if I would like to share the fare to Gatwick where a refugee train was waiting. So we galloped up the old London road, through shadows cast by the majestic viaduct, and finally re-connected to Victoria four hours late.

After the turmoil of the body at Balcombe, things settled back into a grim routine. The worst of it is the silence. Carriages packed with people but no one exchanging a civil word. Until the day a rather shabby old man, unable to find a seat, approached a personable young lady with the unusual opening gambit, "Do you mind if I sit on your lap?" Now we're absolutely prohibited from laughing and singing, and looking is a dodgy option as someone might see you doing it. But hearing remains a hidden freedom; you can pretend to be asleep when all the while tuning into the concert performance of coughing, or the cautionary tale on the perils of unattended luggage. So when the old boy so brazenly broke the ice, ear wax ricocheted about the carriage like a meteor storm. Was he about to open his raincoat and do something regrettable, or was he just the girl's eccentric uncle? Their merry banter continued down the line, Mister Mac making carnal allusion to Crouch End and the girl's voice tinkling merrily; a drôle touch of humanity aboard the Gatwick Express.

Alas, this was a rare diverting interlude. With each succeeding day you struggle to maintain a flicker of perceptive consciousness. A bank shining with daffodils as the train slides through South Croydon; the Thames shimmering in the early morning light. Ultimately, the suffocating emptiness of commuter life smothers your sentient self. The most debilitating stage of my journey is a single stop on the Victoria Line. The train erupts onto the platform and the doors open to reveal a human cargo moulded into the curvaceous shape of the carriage. A few stifled gasps from people hopelessly trying to escape, then the pneumatic seals snap shut and the train thunders off into the swirling heat and dust, the artery of a grumbling volcano. If you're lucky, the train will reach Green Park in one fell swoop, but normally it subsides to a halt in the tunnel, the temperature rising exponentially; the dense air stirred by a salvo of silent but deadly farting.

Today, made for a meeting at the Ministry of Education. Educationalists transpose the thrill of commuting into their working lives; grey, flaccid, lifeless vessels talking in strings of acronyms. There are just three complete words that excite their leaden minds, occasionally combined together in the exultant phrase, 'engaging the stakeholder in conversation.' The fusion of these words acts as a catalyst, generating a range of contorted gestures like battery hens released into sunlight. Then it's back to draining the lifeblood out of agenda item 19; the ceiling sinks, consciousness fades and numbness stills your brain. The faces round the table are bereft of expression, almost immobile, yet still capable of interminable speech. The chief civil servant records every contribution with the deft sweep of a fountain pen. Flanked by a woman in a headscarf and pillar box glasses, chewing and staring blankly like a mesmerised sheep. The wide expanse of window offers a sense of escape. Four crowns on top of Victoria Tower, a pot plant on a lone stem and Westminster Abbey glowing in the golden sunshine. I pick up my backpack, nod farewell to the fountain pen and vault over the school wall.

Back on the packed train carriage, fingers tap dance on keyboards, eyes locked on the omnipotent screen. Bound and wired into solitary shells, cold and detached, features dulled by lack of sleep. Grey light, grey skin, swine flu mutating in the air conditioning system. I have sometimes wondered, but failed to fathom, why anyone should become a dosser. Now I know. Anything – sleeping on cardboard under a leaking railway bridge – anything must be better than the daily grind to the office in London town. The word commute, sometimes used to describe the shortening of a prison term, is in fact a life sentence without a chink of blue sky. I left the train and sat in the window of 'Si Signori', absorbed in the life of Sydney Street. Vibrant colours, spring-heeled feet and a chirpy line in headgear. I pulled on a purple minstrel hat with hanging bells, and wrote my letter of resignation.

***

States of Bliss. A shop front on the sliproad to Rottingdean beach is one man's secret stage. Theatre spotlights above, velvet drapes behind, and all manner of memorabilia on display. The musical score to 'The Teddy Bears' Picnic', a shiny pair of red stiletto shoes and a lively pirate lady, pistol primed in her corset, cutlass in her garter, legs astride an abundant treasure chest. There is no entrance to 'Bliss', but perhaps in the dead of night the stage lights up, the marionettes come to life and the cabaret unfolds.

Next door Eric has moved his Italian café ten metres up the road. Same plastic banquettes, same old menu with ration book prices, same excellent coffee that unzips the roof of your mouth. Italians have a mystical link to authentic coffee. My first job as a school kid was delivering meat for the only non-kosher butcher in North West London. Used to lug great tubs of lard into the 'Bamboo Bar', built into the arches that shook as the trains rolled into Golders Green station. Long before all the froth and nonsense of stylised cups of coffee, a big Italian mama in black shift and scowl held court behind the espresso machine, dispensing awesome cups of coffee and chocolate. We used to take root there at weekends until driven out for some phantom misdemeanour. In these days of permafrost smiles and scripted service, there is something appealing about mein host treating their customers with contempt. Philippe behind the bar at 'Le Bistrot Parisien' in Rouen, projects a morose demeanour, exhausted with life, reciting the dishes of the day like a court usher reading a charge sheet. People queue up to eat there.

***

Down to the old fruit and veg market in Circus Street for an installation of modern art. The whole street is derelict now apart from the 'Market Diner', preserved in the fat of a thousand fried sausages. Confit café. The disused warehouse is prime Corleone territory, grim shafts of light piercing the gloom as a machine gun rattles out retribution. Two young arty types on the door offer advice on the hazards inside; not just gangland revenge but an uneven floor surface and a hole the shape of a giant Easter egg. Evidently health and safety was always with us; a faded sign on the wall counsels barrow boys against travelling faster than 4 mph. Either side of the Easter egg lie two red tree trunks, people circling silently as if in the presence of greatness. A pigeon trapped in the back of the cauliflower department, sends forth a plaintive cooing; probably plain pigeon speak for 'Seen better in a burnt out dovecote.'

The artist Anish Kapoor, redeems himself with another work at the Chattri, the Indian shrine on The Downs beyond Patcham. A great curved shape reflecting the hills and the changing sky. Walk around the other side and the world turns upside down. This is a godawful place to get to; I arrived shredded by a nettle thicket, yet a procession of Brighton folk come to witness the event. Some on shire horses with shaggy feet, others on bikes, babes in buggies, dogs straining at the leash. We appreciate living in a special town and try our best to participate. Back on the Lewes Road, a group of locals are converting the wasteland next to the Co-op into a communal garden. The rabid Alsatian barbed wire fencing is rolled back, and giant segments of concrete pipework are turned into painted flower pots. Rubbish cleared, soil laid and plants bedded in a pagan circle as wistful notes from an accordion float above the traffic. If the banks finally crumble and corporations crash, we will still manage to live off rabbits from The Downs, sole from the sea and vegetables grown to the sound of music.

***

Yesterday Brighton hosted a naked bike ride in protest against the motor car. The thought of speeding along, scrotum chafing against the saddle, is a concept too far, so I headed West to Shoreham, suitably protected in shorts and navy blue under crackers. Could not help but notice a procession of cyclists coming the other way, all remarkably similar in stature. Stocky, bull-like necks, serious helmets rammed over solid heads. Like Fritz the motorcade rider, just before the Ober-Lieutenant in the sidecar copped the full force of a bouncing bomb. Some of the procession looked a little misshapen in cycle wear; snug-fit lycra is not designed for beefy hanging breasts. But all carried a look of wonderment on their faces, delight at having escaped the tyranny of the car, discovering a whole new world within sound and scent of the sea.

To avoid the murderous lorries on the main coastal route, I took the slip road to the sea lock. A featureless stretch of beach broken by a lone jetty, occasionally glistening with surfers, and on the other side, gravel yards shunted into giant cones and pyramids. The lock path remained stubbornly shut as a stream of yachts trundled by on their weekend constitutional. No risk of unfurling a sail or breaking through the waves; just time to talk nautical talk, uncork the bubbly then head back to the mooring. A plume of mist drifted in from the sea and my mind melted into oblivion. Eventually the lock gates swung to, the line of bikes and push chairs filed across, and I made for the Farmers' Market.

Until recently, decent local produce barely existed in this country, but now every second Saturday of the month, Shoreham presides over a feast of food and drink. High Weald sheep cheese, Twineham Grange parmesan and Nut Knowle goat cheese rolled in ash. Chutneys, relishes, honey and pies, wine and cider, fish from Rye. Every cut of game and meat, the entire pig including hock and feet. Prize tomatoes smelling sharp and sweet. Scrumptious Sussex apples. The surprising thing is how quickly your behaviour changes in response to the market. Content to queue with anticipation for the current crop of vegetables. Smelling this and tasting that, exchanging smiles and conversation. All as if supermarkets belonged to some alien past where we lost control of our lives.

Across the pedestrian bridge, several houseboats open their doors to displays of art. These are hippy places in the best sense of the word. No spineless souls, slumped smelling of cats, incapable of making a roll up between one solstice and the next. But craftsmen, designers of fantasy beach huts. Psychedelic shapes on sepia mud flats. Back in the centre of town, art is also on display at Rope Tackle, a new complex built on the site of a derelict wharf. A mosaic of wood and brick with pretty blue balconies, and four metal trees stretching up in static dance around a bold, glass staircase. On the quayside, water churns darkly at the confluence of river and sea, trains rattle across the estuary, and swans bob about, humourless and tight-beaked. Sniffing contemptuously at the hippies on the houseboats.

***

A collection of Merchant Ivory characters transposed to a Normandy garden. There to celebrate 'le vernissage', the opening of an exhibition of engravings. My friend Dominique bought an impression of a dark and brooding potato. Another lady unhinged something quite indecipherable off the wall; Norman houses must have big attics. A wonderful array of faces squeezed under the gazebo as the rain cloud burst. Two grey sisters with untethered hair and vague smiles revealing magnificent buck teeth. Three fay men, one with the studied look of the anguished French artist, eyes rolled into his head, dark thoughts casting shadows across his brow. Whether to plunge now, head first into the septic tank, or wait for a more delicious moment. The second in blue blazer and unlit cob pipe, conversing silently with himself, and the third, the absolute image of Len Fairclough. Widely reported as dead after that unseemly interlude in the swimming baths and a seismic spat with Elsie Tanner, I can reveal Len alive, if somewhat subdued, staring dreamily from the whicker sofa. Wedged between two widows, husbands just departed, one deeply amorous with her pup, the other in an auburn hair bubble that must have meant months at the barbers. Then there is 'Le Danois', strange object of Dominique's desire, every bland utterance bringing forth a flutter of laughter. The whole gathering presided over by a game old lady with cane and humpback, each word articulated up and down like Captain Pugwash. Owner of the tumbledown château and grounds, including a diminutive outhouse that is home to grandson Simon. I imagine serious money funds the whole estate, but Simon displays none of the privilege of Grande École or Polytechnique, just a woolly hat haircut and the muffled grunting of modern youth.

Dominique runs a fine guest house. Deep sleep beds, palatial windows and walls of ancient books. Giant bath tubs awash with bubbles. Breakfast is a thing of wonderment. Warm, nutty bread, thick yoghurt doused in honey and whatever sumptuous fruit the season has in store. Coffee from one of those octagonal numbers that hiss and cackle on the stove. Bright cardboard figures dance around the breakfast table which looks out onto the bell towers of old Rouen. If ever you visit this historic city, and you must, then book into 'Chambre Avec Vue.'

When I was resident in Rouen, La Maison de Mule had an even more commanding view. The Seine winding through fields from the East, disappearing behind the spires of the city, then finally reflecting a sunset between banks of industrial chimneys. A new bridge is being built across the river, able to levitate when the tall ships hit town. The technology involved probably cost a billion euros, but that is the French state, accommodating an Armada that docks for ten days every five years. All the galleries of Rouen contain images of the ancient ships, but I have been captured by the evolving bridge. First the two giant towers on either bank, then the section straddling the water and finally the segments of road slotted together like a giant Scalextric set. Can't wait to pedal across it.

***

A vast swarm of catering workers climbing the steps to Ascot, like a football crowd filling the terraces. Two distinct team strips, waiters in black and white, chefs in hats and check trousers. There are various clans within the crowd. A hard core of chefs who reconvene each summer to work 'the circuit' of sporting events. Then the old retainers, front of house, waistcoated waiters with deferential blood running through pale blue veins. And game old geese with fantastic perms, soon to reach that great doily in the sky, clutching a serving fork and spoon. And there's us, the catering college brigade, excitable and away from home, bottom rung on the kitchen ladder, hulling fields of strawberries and running errands up spiral stairs. A first taste of the hospitality industry, hot and hierarchical.

At the top, head chefs garnered from all the great race courses and stadiums of England. Adept at keeping a hundred dishes spinning in the air; deftly bringing one down while setting another in motion. Directing supplies from the central hub to twenty satellite kitchens. Some dispensing the vitriol that scarred them as a commis, others contrary to common belief, remaining calm and genial. Supported by a band of second chefs, canny and indispensable. Quietly pulling off conjuring tricks when a batch of salmon goes missing, or when a mean, spindly, malevolent guest invents a new food allergy. Then comes a disparate group of chefs, who have yet to really make it. Some embroidering their lives with outrageous flights of fantasy; an expanding realm of real estate or filming with celebrities. An unnerving stare, a machine gun laugh betraying some inner calamity. But their existence is as paradise compared to the kitchen porter, the rung beneath the ladder immersed in greasy water. Unspoken in our fair country, apartheid dark as night. Every porter at Ascot wore a black face, the toffs in tails wore white.

Each night we were bused back to an imposing Gothic building at Egham. Half public school – quads, statues and giant portraits staring down in the halls. Half nuthouse, each door with a little spy hole, and the windows barred from opening. The rooms were identically numbered around each quad, and the stairs and walkways ran in such confusing fashion, you were always in danger of barging into a stranger's bedroom. Three old fashioned bathtubs on each floor, the pipes primed with scorching water. Ravenous after a hard day's work, the food was tepid and bitter. Breaded chicken every night with frozen sweetcorn for veg, and frozen sweetcorn for salad. Perhaps it was the folly of the architecture, or the depraved diet, but despite the arduous work each day I have never laughed so much. It was like living in a J.P. Donleavy creation, butlers walking the parapets, exploding hearths and swinging candelabras. Pindi and Peggy laughed in that open African way, cheeks shining, often collapsing to the floor in a rolling state of paroxysm. Pleading for release from merriment, sackcloth and sobriety. In a world burbling with phones, stuck in a tunnel, drooping with shopping, patched up with pills, glued to a screen, nagging concern that the climate's gone missing... how good it is to simply rock back your head, open your muzzle and roar.

Bused back in the final day, after an ill-advised night at the pub. The only sound of life on the coach was the gaggle of old retainers, still unable to comprehend how this year the terminus was 'Car Park 5.' Ever since buses were preceded by a man waving a red flag, the waiters have unloaded at 'Car Park 2.' 'Car Park Fiiiive', enunciated in a slow, bovine drawl, anathema to the concept of innovation. The drama of the change complemented by an emphatic mime of all available digits. In days of yore the reward for working yourself into the ground was a case of bubbly and a haunch of venison. Head chefs built extensions on the proceeds of liberated food and drink. Today, with security guards on every corner and computerised stock control, you leave the premises with zilch. The bins groaning with prime produce as you travel back famished.

***

When does it happen that you disconnect from youth? You can grow up at the height of punk, pogo to The Damned, the spotlight projecting a volley of phlegm at Dave Vannions' pallid face. Squeeze into the bogs, with Tiny the giant skinhead on one side and Adam Ant on the other. Seek out every Buzzcocks gig, rejoicing as the stalls are reduced to fire wood, the bouncers tossed aside like puppets, the crowd invading the stage to a supercharged version of 'Fiction Romantic.' Still clubbing well past your sell-by date, spirit untrammelled, lithe and impetuous. At what stage then, did youth become an alien presence – lolling along on million dollar trainers soon to be slung over telegraph wires, trousers hanging below undercrackers, fatties exposing their anal crack? When did life settle for the quiet of a deep pile carpet, the bubble of wine in the potting shed, putting on your reading glasses and turning the pages of Monet at The Tate? And when will the imperceptible process transmute into crabby old age, patrolling the banning orders on Hove Lawns, no football on the grass, no parties on the beach, no modern architecture to shatter the horizon? Last night at a Philharmonic concert at The Dome, the man in front groaned, an exasperated Gordon Brown god I'm miserable now groan, when an anarchic scattering of enthusiasts broke into applause between movements. Are we condemned to lose touch with the vibrant effervescence of Brighton and retreat to the flat barren lands West of the Old Pier where the wind gathers up the sighs and moans to fuel a procession of glowering waves? Or will we dye our stubbly hair terra cotta and promenade along the beach in stripy Edwardian bathing wear, brightening our twilight days with a mischievous sense of sparklement?

***

They call Rouen 'The Sleeping Giant' as the city does little to promote its golden heritage to the outside world. A stunning cathedral, a hundred bell towers, streets of tumbledown timbered houses. The spire of L'église Jeanne d'Arc, stretching across the cobblestones like a pterodactyl tail. Le Palais de Justice, once darkly Gothic beneath a brooding sky, now restored to shining splendour with elegant turrets and pop-eyed gargoyles. The whole façade sculpted with extravagant flourish, like the fantasy confection of a master pastry chef. This is far too fine a place to condemn men to the cells. Behold, Jean Genet and his fugitive lover, dragging their chains up the stone stairs, bestriding the balcony and demanding release to a life of theft and debauchery. Casting red and black roses into the air they captivate the crowd who storm the courtyard with a primal roar, shedding the cold, mean, Norman mistrust that has curdled the milk of human kindness for centuries or more:

"Liberty! Fraternity!

"Set the Wild Men free!"

Well in August, the Giant sinks further into subterranean sleep. Humphrey Bogart could check into town with Lauren Bacall slung over his shoulder, and no one would know as all the Rouennais have left for the beach. Stuck in the middle of August, Le Quinze Août is a public 'holiday' with all the animation of a funeral cortège on silent film. A lone bell tolls, dead leaves chase around the courtyard, and a few deserted tourists spin slowly in the void. The animation of the food market evaporates into the sky. Empty aisles of unclaimed lettuce, steaming bins of fish bones and a few old timers sampling second hand books. Even the chicken seller, normally so boisterous in front of his spit, turns his cry of 'Poulet! Poulet!' into a slow, halting lament. Rats sniff in the gutter, gulls eyeball the rats, Le Gros Horloge shuts its eyes and time stands still.

The coastal resorts of Normandy move at a quiet pace. Waves sifting the shingle with a metronomic hush, gulls serenading fishermen as they untangle their catch. Up on the wooded cliff tops, the tranquil village of Varengeville offers simple delights. The ruined Château of Jean Ango, with a view commanding his mighty fleet. The rose garden of Le Parc des Moutiers, protected from the sea by towering trees. Down in the valley, Pourville is a little line of beach huts between two great cliffs. One crazy golf course, two tennis courts, but nothing to do when the weather breaks. The oyster farm provides little in the way of interactive fun, the oysters catatonic and stubbornly tight-lipped. Best to push the boat out at 'Produits Fruits de Mer', a pearl of a restaurant run by LeBon, father and son, for the past sixty years. Ceremonial silence accompanies the laying of cutlery for the seafood tour de force. A nut cracker for the crab claws, a pronger for the whelks and a needle to crucify the cockles. Throw in basketfuls of bread, lashings of mayonnaise, a bottle of crisp white wine and the feast is complete.

A tot of old Calva to clear a space before the local cheeses. Pont l'Evêque and Livarot are both good when warm as freshly baked bread. But the prize cheese is

Neufchatel, named after the little market town in the heart of the Pays de Bray. Neufchatel is a taste explosion, blowing the roof off your head. Patched up and sedated, you have to go back for more. The perfect cheese is meltingly ripe, maturity taking the edge off the cordite, leaving your tongue intact. The last Neufchatel I bought smelt and tasted of the farmyard. A live, almost carnal food, rich and deeply authentic. Tucked away in the hills near Bellencombre, snowy white goats command your affection as they clamour and roll in the hay. This is where the Bazin family make their famous 'chèvre.' Ladled into moulds, and rolled in ash, it bears no resemblance to the sharp, acidic mass-produced logs. Sun-kissed on a summer picnic, the skin barely manages to contain its creamy centre. If ever there was a cheese like nectar, then this is it.

***

I love the Co-op on the Lewes Road. One size up from those corner Co-ops sparsely stocked with spam and marrow fat peas, this shop has everything you ever need beyond goose liver and asses' milk. There's an honest simplicity about the place: three aisles, staff that never leave and no-nonsense labelling: 'These eggs come from caged hens.' Recently they've introduced Co-op radio, and you find yourself transported down the aisle with The Stone Roses, swinging your wire basket to 'I wanna be adored.' As near as it gets in middle age to a fun night on the dance floor. Last week, goodies packed and ready for the off, the Turkish girl on the till asked me to respond with a confidential click; had I found the service to be excellent? Larder stocked in minutes without the bamboozlement of infinite choice, last litre of Coppella apple juice snuffled from under the nose of a dreamy student and re-acquaintance with 'Enola Gay.' Excellent is too small a word. Award that Turk the freedom of Brighton and the Bosphorus.

Barbers are opening up all along the Lewes Road. You wouldn't think there was enough hair to go around, although on reflection the less you have the more you need it tended, scything off those stray antennae, like Brillo barbs on a coconut. 'Quick Kutz' the new Afro emporium, has a menu including 'Extreme Patterns'; enter the shop as Kojak, walk out Marge Simpson. There's a certain protocol in the barber shop. Seat yourself on the bench, open 'The Sun', and join in the conversation ping ponging between lacquered heads and masters of cutting edge satire. It's like the philosophy department of a talk show twinned with the wisdom of a taxi driver. Eventually it is my turn to be wrapped in the chair, and I ask for a Number 2 all over. There are certain dark corners of Brighton where this request could land you in a sticky fix. 'Dukes Mound' is the nocturnal venue for such events, every fetish and fandango paraded among the bushes. Imagine my surprise when cycling innocently by I noticed a spanking new villa on top of the hill. I peered through the window at wifey busy painting, and walked over to hubbie sawing away, engaged in a bit of do it yourself. Yes, the derelict building had been restored, and smitten by the view they had just moved in. What a view, he said, as our heads turned out to sea. The poor sap, soon to be devoured by wolves. Off to walk the dog one night, as the missus crochets a cushion cover; a canine whimper, a rude embrace, ensnared by a troupe of Frank N. Furters.

The whole Rocky Horror circus descends on the 'Theatre Royal' each year, nine hundred transvestites belting out 'The Time Warp'; the delicate pillars of the grand 'Old Lady' shaking to the chorus. The theatre began life in a barn on the Old Steine, the actors having to exit stage left when the harvest arrived. Two hundred years ago, it moved to the present site on New Road, and fifty years later Phipps the architect raised the roof to create The Gallery, with a ceiling bordered like an exquisite wedding cake. A narrow staircase leads to the fireplace in Mrs Nyechart's parlour, now the 'Balcony Bar', a huge bay window offering an unblemished view of the Pavilion gardens and those wacky turban rooftops.

Backstage, fishermen performed the role of 'flymen', hauling the ropes that raised the giant backdrops to a play, mending their nets between scene changes, then off for a night's fishing. 'Flying matinées' arrived with the railways, an entire company – actors, props and all – jumping on the London train to make the evening performance. The whole building is filled with creaking passages and curiosities. The two prime dressing rooms are numbered 1 and 1a so as not to offend the sensibilities of the stars. A little hatch leads from the wings to the Colonnade Bar, a snug corner hung with velvet drapes and theatre lights, the model of a Maître D doffing his top hat to the passers-by, and photos of ancient actors gazing down with detached serenity.

Outside, New Road has become Brighton Boulevard, beautifully paved, devoid of cars, magnificent wooden benches winking through the night. Once in a while the Council allow a farmers' market to take over the street, an abundance of Sussex produce vibrant with taste and vitality. A stark contrast to the desert that has encroached upon the nearby library, the magnificent glass facade which once mirrored the rooftops of the Dome, now plunged into darkness by monuments to corporate eating. The man who runs the farmers' market has his office in Ship Street Gardens, a narrow brick-paved alleyway just up from the beach. There's an old time 'Caff' and an 'Erotic Boutique' with thigh-length leather boots, so seriously clasped and buckled they would prop you up when legless. The window of an antique warehouse filled with memorabilia. A pile of ancient books bound inside a bell jar, the pages so dark and fragile they would turn to dust at the blink of an eye. A 'Pye' wireless, with one band receiving the 'Third' and 'Light' programmes, another travelling through a sea of static sound, to impossibly distant destinations – Cairo, Ankara, Reykjavik, Atlantica. At Festival time this street might come alive with dancers dressed as bumble bees, and a group of avid citizens bustling by on the tour of 'Famous Brighton Back Passages.' Herein lies the conundrum for our town. Whether the streets of Brighton retain the unpredictable humour and colour of the sea, or succumb to death by blandness; the chain store massacre.

***

Wandered through Dieppe with time to kill before the ferry, so popped into a bar in the 'Le Pollet' district. Just a few washed out faces eking out their glasses of 'pression' or 'pastis'. La patronne was surprisingly young and lively, blond, quite voluptuous really. Hard to imagine what kept her in this drab little backwater where no one in a lifetime had ventured beyond the rising bridge. All of a sudden she became quite animated, searching for the name of a chestnut brown flower. None of the regulars could help her and she disappeared up a staircase in search of inspiration. Difficult to know what provided the answer to her quest; an internet connection is a millennium away. Probably the local wise woman who doubles as a midwife is stashed away in the attic. Anyway, she returned glowing, revealing the name of the plant: 'Le désespoir des poètes' (1). Only the French could name a plant thus. Despair is a tangible feature of their life. In English schools children learn to write an essay with a beginning, a middle and an end. In France it's a beginning, a middle and a suicide pact. Round the corner there's another bar, 'Mieux ici qu'en face' (2). I've come to the conclusion that Brighton offers a warmer, happier existence than the Norman side of the Channel. But these quirky episodes of French life have a quality all of their own.

(1) 'Poets' despair'
(2) 'Better here than over there'

***

Travel upstairs on a Brighton bus and you are on display. The wide band of windows reveals serried ranks of passengers travelling into town, waving and singing as the driver takes a turn around the Old Steine. Big images of local heroes are printed on the side of each bus; a cool clubbing dude, a jogging grandad, a supermum juggling triplets. All on the crest of an acid trip, beaming above the caption, 'Yes! We're on the Bus!' The real experience is a little different, passengers ricocheting down the gangway at each touch of the brakes, desperately avoiding eye contact with the crazed old critter poised to chat, finally slumping down next to a big melting jellyfish oozing a terrible stench. If you thought you'd seen the last of stinking people with that pale boy in primary school who persisted in pissing himself; be assured, they remain legion on board the bus. Open a window to dilute the smell and a hidden hand slams it shut, asserting their right to travel in suffocating heat.

The back of the bus informs every motorist, 'We're busy shopping while you're stuck in traffic', when of course no one is shopping, we're all stuck in traffic. The bus fuming in gridlock, inching forward painfully with each jarring squeal of the brakes. Catch a lung full of the black exhaust as you weave by on your bike; it's got to do you good. Any Town Hall worth its salt would have pedestrianised the town centre, banned the car and laid tramways north, east and west. Then travel might really be a cause for waving and singing. The great thing is that despite the congestion, the feral kids and the stifling heat, we always thank the driver at the moment of escape. Give us a proper transport system and we would garland him with flowers, bestow Belgian chocolates, indulge in fond embrace.

The trains are trying to get it right, sometimes dawdling at a station because they've arrived ahead of time. Recently travelled east for the Scallop Festival at Rye, the conductor dispensing joviality up and down the carriage, his announcements over the public address delivered with the emollient diction of Jeeves. 'The trolley will be proceeding down the aisle serving Pimms and caviar kettle crisps.' He even managed to placate an eruption of Italian students at Eastbourne, transforming a loco commotion into something approaching calm. If you ever wondered why there are no tea shops in Brighton, the answer is they have all migrated to Rye, every other latticed window offering crumpets and sticky toffee pudding. The alternate windows are restaurants of fine repute, and I settled into the 'Ypres Castle' for a plate of scallops and a glass of fruity Biddenden wine. Then down to the Fish Market to snuffle a dozen more scallops back to Brighton; some things are just too good to leave behind.

Half a dozen boats were snuggled up to a curve on the River Tillingham, neat and sparkling in the winter sun. Threadbare flags tugging at the mast like bedraggled pirate headgear. The river winding through green fields, quite unlike the setting at Brighton Marina where I set sail the next day. The harbour walls deep, barren and grey like the womb of a nuclear submarine. Clouds hung over the cliffs rising and falling towards Rottingdean, shining bravely through the gloom. Alan's plucky little boat cutting through the waves, finding the buoy and hauling in the nets. No easy harvest as a glistening catch tumbled into the hold, but each fish tightly enmeshed by tooth and gill, trapped in a final act of defiance. Sole, plaice and a magnificent sea bass, eventually freed, sighing at the bottom of the boat in a blood-stained coat of chain mail.

Back at the quayside, the fish were stacked in boxes marked 'Surprise', the name of the boat that spirited Charles the Second to France in 1651. Skipper Nicholas Tettersell received £60 for his troubles, and after returning from exile Charles rewarded him with enough sovereigns to buy the Old Ship Inn. The Old Ship still stands on the seafront, blissfully untainted by functional modern design. A maze of grumbling floorboards leading to the ornamental finesse of the Paganini suite. Wood panelled walls suddenly parting as the ghost of a linen trolley trundles by. Steep stone stairs descending to a warren of chalk tunnels lit by flickering torches. Vaulted cellars where accounts of income and expenditure are recorded in beautifully scripted ledgers, all stoutly bound in burgundy red. The hotel embodies the history of the town, once the principal coaching house, set among hemp fields harvested for fishing nets. The Prince Regent entertained here, trays circulating with devilled kidneys and Madeira as the royal dragoon guards staged battles on the cliff. One day in July 1821, the whole town made for The Level to celebrate the Prince's coronation, and with all eyes turned the other way, the Old Ship filled with a catch of smuggled gin.

Today the flag above the hotel hangs in shreds, torn by a terrible storm. A waitress peers through the salt-stained windows, as the waves rage like a Medieval army rampaging at the city gates. Sea and sky embroiled together in a tempestuous whirl of grey. The waves effortlessly climbing the shingle beach, like a lion devouring its prey, shaking its mane in an awesome show of strength. Then just when the Arches lie frozen at its mercy, the beast laughs and settles back into its lair. Leaving a portent of chaotic times to come, when the glaciers melt into molten seas, promenading couples are swept off their feet and the Old Ship floats away.

**

The hidden trick in catering is good organisation, but all too often restaurants run in a state of mayhem, staff stretched to the limit, the sink blocked, the KP walking out, service teetering on the edge of the abyss. I have just experienced three chaotic days, in a fading seafront hotel deep in Hove, requisitioned by orthodox Jews to celebrate the festival of Passover. I got changed and trying to exit the toilet 'suite', the door handle came away and unravelled on the floor. I hammered and stomped, eventually summoning someone on the other side who prized open the catch. Had I known what was in store, I would have stayed sitting quietly, counting time on the pot.

The kitchen was being cleansed by two rabbis, fiendishly scouring the place with boiling water and branding the surfaces with red hot irons. When finally it was deemed fit for work, they loitered furtively, ready to stymie my every movement with a bizarre biblical edict. Light the oven with a candle borne in a glass. Pour the chicken soup into a pot bound with bull rushes while pounding your feet and chest. In this scenario Gary Rhodes would have been hard pressed to serve up a decent dinner, but the kitchen was presided over by a lumbering porpoise of a man, each portion of his body pulled in opposing directions as fresh crises broke over his head. He appeared to comply with every rabbinical diktat while secretly engaging in acts of subterfuge so that meals might somehow arrive on time. A hooded Pole sent under cover for supplies of forbidden fruit. Soup blended in an outhouse, defying the rules of the Sabbath.

Even without divine interference the kitchen was unbelievably cramped and ill-equipped. An abiding image of the Porpoise floundering to save the food on a makeshift table as it folded on spindly legs. All the while issuing orders like Captain Bligh on a tilting deck. Worse still, he answered to the name of Malcolm. Gentiles can be cool as Malcolm. Malcolm McLaren, Malcolm Allison shredding a super-sized cigar between his teeth, and that ravishing Malcolm in a 'A Clockwork Orange'. Jewish Malcolms live with their mother, and are sent off to work with a fresh pair of pants and an M&S label sticking out of their neck, 'If lost or found out late, please send my son home.'

The third morning he appeared with such deeply ringed eyes, like the tortured boss of Inspector Clouseau, or Avram Grant as Abramovich wielded the axe. Perversely he tried to lighten the atmosphere with a terrible joke; at my expense. I did the merciful thing, branded him on the forehead with the scalding iron and folded him into the freezer to rest in peace with the turkeys. The rabbi concurred with this sequence of events, counseled me against coveting my neighbour's ass, then pottered quietly away. Doubt and apprehension casting shadows across his face.

What is it about this industry that produces pandemonium? My favourite tale comes from a friend who worked in a coffee shop on Oxford High Street. Disgusted with the owners' exploitative practices, the entire crew spontaneously jumped ship, leaving the customers untended, free to rifle the till and gorge themselves on cake. Somewhere there is a modicum of order, where the head chef does not collapse in a pile of whisky bottles behind the bins, and the KP does not empty the contents of the mop bucket down the salad sink. As a catering student I interviewed Anton Mosiman, then head chef at The Dorchester. On the wall of his office, the entire kitchen brigade, standing in ranks like a school photograph. I imagined him inspecting the staff each morning, adjusting a neckerchief here, a toque there, the equipment immaculate and humming gently. A picture so rare and strange as to achieve the status of myth.

***

They're burning tyres on the bridges across the Seine. Traffic backed up for miles, each driver sealed into a capsule of despair as the thick acrid smoke seeps through the air conditioning. The café terraces shake their heads in resignation, resignation tinged with pride at La France, a refined state of order always bubbling on the edge of rebellion. The terraces like fickle football supporters, ready to bend towards any convenient response. An emphatic shrug of disgust at the French malaise if surrounded by sharp-suited modernisers, then swept up by a crowd in caps and blue overalls, unfurling adherence to the proletarian banner, demanding the dignity of life beyond the market place. We're in this together even if we have to starve in the process. I remember returning from a demo against Le Pen, and there, not on the march but installed on a banquette in the 'Bistrot Parisienne', was an actress with startling cheekbones, expounding her impeccable cobblestone credentials. Grandpapa, stubbornly resisting Franco in the Spanish Civil War, and papa driving De Gaulle into exile during the heady days of 1968. Confusingly, the French word for actress is 'comedienne', and when I asked her to 'tell us a joke', she dismissed me with a regal turn of the head, sipped on a green Diablo and continued her revolutionary tale. The next day the ferry slipped out of Dieppe unopposed, the blockade of fishermen having melted away to bolster that other French tradition now under threat, the goodly lunch. Fire in the belly rekindled around a sumptuous 'pot au feu.'

***

I have paid homage at White Hart Lane since the age of nine. Suffered, roared, been torn apart, seen Stevie Perryman raise the UEFA Cup shining beneath the flood lights, Hoddle dipping a volley over Shilton and Chivers in his pomp, leaving donkey defenders for dead. As a kid I used to take the 102 bus from the ghetto, file through the clickety click gates, set up shop in front of a crush barrier behind the Paxton Road goal, stand on my handmade stool and wait for the teams to appear. Bus fare, match ticket, programme and still have change from half a crown for a bag of monkey nuts. Pre-match practice was not the high octane affair of the modern game orchestrated by men in Michelin suits, but Jimmy Greaves ambling out, nonchalantly chewing gum, stubbing out his fag on the goal post and caressing a few shots at Pat Jennings. When more serious business ensued he always seemed to score by striking low into the corner of the goal, the ball nestling against the stanchion. Just occasionally he indulged in something more spectacular, breaking clear of the Liverpool defence before crashing the ball into the net, two converging red giants left in a heap of scrap metal. Game over, the terraces would cascade out of the ground, and we would run through bomb sites that remained bare and gaping for generations, across Bruce Grove Park and await a lift home in the neat back-to-back streets of the Peabody Estate. The park was always crossed at a gallop, don't know why, that was the tradition, even Uncle Harold with a dodgy ticker summoned up a trot, pausing for breath outside the corner shop with a radio loudspeaker, relaying results from across the land. Euphoria was news of Ian Ure sinking The Arse with an own goal off his knee. Then home for Victory Kippers.

Until today I had never been to the ground when there wasn't a match, but the Club advertised the Tottenham Carnival, so I decided to take a look. In the park those giant dead trees of winter have been brought to life with vibrant rose beds and competing sound systems. The event seriously carved up by security. Search your bag, search for your knife, more men in neon jackets than you could shake a stick at. The castle in the park was built by Robert the Bruce, then confiscated by Edward the Second, peeved at him pinching Scotland. Inside there is all manner of historic information, the village of Tottenham valued in the Domesday book at 25 pounds, 15 shillings and 3 ounces of gold. Barely enough to shine Jermaine Defoe's boots.

In Tottenham High Street three milestones to the match stand closed and silent. The civic toilets, the 'Corner Pin' pub, and 'Glickman the Ironmongers', where the last in a line of Glickmans still respects the sanctity of half day closing. Established in 1932, the shopfront lists an inventory of household names from the past:

'Hoes, rakes, spades and shears'.

'Padlocks, hinges and bolts'.

Norman, Mackay, Beal and Knowles.

Hoddle, Ardiles and Crooks.

Tottenham is populated with poor people from every corner of the world, but for food as with football, there are reasons for hope. Grocers abundant with exotic fruit and vegetables. The fleeting appearance of a great little Thai café with 'Monsoon Wine'. And 'Cirric' a Turkish restaurant, just a goal kick from the Park Lane end, better than anything on the South Coast. You are drawn in by the intoxicating aroma from an enormous wood grill, the smouldering ashes crowned with a majestic copper hood. Every meal is accompanied with sumptuous salad, a plate of chargrilled onions in pomegranate juice, and the most compulsively tasty bread. Flat, chewy and sun-smoked on that magic grill. On match days it is mayhem in here, a confusion of orders, people queuing anxiously to partake before kick off. Today I am the lone customer, and the waitress brings me extra scorched onions and more freshly baked bread. I try in vain to extract the bread recipe, but it is sealed in the tomb of the ancient Ottoman Gastronome. The waitress knows Brighton (great) and Crawley (less great). Better still was last night's Euro match when Turkey stood tall to beat Croatia on penalties. I explain that the star Croatian played for Tottenham, and try to describe Luka Modrić. Young, slim, flowing hair. A sign of recognition lights up her face, and suddenly shedding all national allegiance, she enquires, "Has he got a wife?"

***

Mother of Mule is down to stay, and we take the bus to The Seven Sisters. Top deck, front seat and an unblemished view of the sea. Not a journey for people pushed for time though. The bus chugs up and down dean, then judders to a halt as the drivers exchange the baton in a backwater of Newhaven, and a whole recalibration of mirrors and ticketing takes place before the colossus trundles off again. Getting on board becomes an Olympian feat as Eastbourne approaches. The Stena step is lowered, the abyss crossed, and a celebratory cannon fires 'Hurrah' from Beachy Head.

The little River Cuckmere winds its way through a gateway to The Downs, and embraces a tranquil sea. A procession of waves march in, flourish their petticoats and peel away, like troupers at the 'Folies Bergere'. 'The Seven Sisters' shares its name with the ferry that carries us to Dieppe. The four hours pass easily, time lost between slumber and a cheeky bottle of Macon Blanc Villages. The cliffs of the 'Côte d'Ivoire' draw into focus, the harbour walls are breached and a man in gauntlets that last did service at Agincourt, lassoes the ship to the quay. Bikes mercifully disembark before the army of container lorries can summon up the toxic fog that propels them up the ramp, over the cliff and away.

The sister ship, 'La Côte d'Alabatre', lies redundant on a desolate dock, where conveyor belts disgorge scallops amid a mountain of stinking shells. This unpromising spot is home to 'La Chaloupe', an outstanding 'routier' restaurant. Join the jovial barney around the 'hors d'oeuvres' table, then tuck into a main course that might be 'lapin au moutarde' or local skate. Savour a choice of Normandy cheeses, find room for a pud, and help yourself to as much Longueville cider as the onward journey permits. All for just a tenner. The clientele are solid working men, wearing their blue overalls like a badge of pride. One humongously muscled brute sways in, barbells bouncing off his biceps, walnuts crushed between his nuts. Accompanied by a divinely pretty boy with sensuous mouth and strawberry blond hair. Madame leads them to an exclusive little room out the back: Notre-Dame-des-Pêcheurs.

Isabelle at the 'Plage Hotel' bristles with delight. The 'pissoir' has been resurrected in Dieppe. At the fish market and on The Prom, two old-time urinals have been installed. No fear of losing a finger in a Venus flytrap coin machine, just the freedom of pointing Percy at the wall and performing like a donkey. Some accommodation has been made to modern hygiene mania, with an automatic flushing device where previously the piss lay stagnant for centuries. A mutant jellyfish with crazed eye in the middle of its forehead, powerless in the privy. Alas, the primeval turd pot, with two raised steps above the abyss, has been deemed beyond recall. For a Number 2 you have to take your chances with the girlies inside the lunar capsule with a sliding door that portends 'You may be sealed inside this space for a very long time.'

All of which should be worthy of record at the Fishing Museum in Hastings, where the 'Rules of the Winkle Club' are prominently displayed:

'Any member having lost his winkle shall receive another at the Club Room by paying 6d.'

In the spirit of cross-cultural collaboration, this protocol should be welded to the urinal at Dieppe. I will make representations to the Mairie on my next visit. Currently though, I am absorbed in family life on Brighton Beach. Four months of torrential rain have driven the seafront traders to religion, acts of sabotage and pounding on the doors of the local Nuthouse, pleading asylum in a padded cell. But now the sky has cleared, a gentle breeze tempers the summer sun, and crowds funnel out of the station, drawn hypnotically by the scent of the sea. A pale flabby couple struggle with a shelter that will stake their claim to the beach. Painfully coaxing a rod inside a stubborn sheath, tension mounts in the shoulder blades, frustration breaks and they flounce down onto the pebbles, each one looking askance at the sea. A quiet shrug, and they set to again, finally producing a semi igloo in two-tone PVC, scarlet and cerise, fluttering bravely above the waves. Now what to do with the remainder of their day?

A bright little family set up camp beside me. Mama goose tending the flock, papa resplendent in Hollywood shades, two voluptuous mermaid daughters, and mother-in-law. Solid shoes and socks, buttoned up cardigan, she looks suspiciously at the clear blue sky and perches on the edge of her deckchair like Mr Punch digesting a suspect sausage. The girls casually perform the swimsuit dance without any sign of distress, mama unpeels her matelot top and papa wantonly exposes his bonce to the unforgiving sun. The womenfolk have a little spat over who should pay the deckchair boy, Nana finally tossing a couple of coins onto the pebbles. To be rescued that night by a man who gathers the glinting harvest when the tourist tide retreats. 'The Beachcomber' is the sign above a Shoreham hairdresser on a little parade of shops soon to be linked to the new pedestrian bridge. The Norman turret of St Mary's de Haura rising at one end, fantasy houseboats at the other. Shoreham is the coming place.

***

When I lived in Rouen my rooftop flat was wedged between 'La Vache Folle', an accomplished hag who recorded every coming and going with malicious intent, and the artist in the attic, Lionel Lagrange. His little turning staircase filled with canvases of masts and clippers, snapshots from the last time the tall ships came to town. Now on the quayside for 'L'Armada', I spot Lionel through the crowd, absorbed behind his easel, oblivious to the fanfare surrounding 'Cuauhtemoc', a magnificent Mexican vessel gliding up the Seine to the stirring sound of 'Carmina Burana.' A hundred sailors line the yards of the three great masts, shoulders entwined like a towering circus act. The crowd cheer as the ship sidles up to its berth, the sailors jump down on deck, and the two sides embrace in a semaphore of flashing phones.

I used to love the desolation of the docks, cycling across abandoned railway tracks, past the avenue of blackened trees to giant cranes transporting wheat in a billowing cloud of dust. Today the quayside is thronging with life, the new bridge 'Le Pont Flaubert', rising to salute the flotilla of maritime greats. An enormous Italian ship, 'Amerigo Vespucci' takes centre stage on the Left Bank, the profile of rigging lit up at night by a firework display, the acoustics ricocheting across the river like cannon fire. Later still, the facade of the cathedral plays host to a 'son et lumière spectacle – Monet aux Pixels.' Those cathedral walls, hewn by convicts from cliffs on the Seine, hoisted on planks and pulleys, scorched by fire and Allied bombs, now restored to pristine splendour, the statues clothed in fresh white robes, reflecting the dappled images of Impressionist art.

The next morning, as scribe to the city, I am treated to a personal tour of HMS Southampton, here on a valedictory visit before pulling on pipe and slippers down a quiet Solent backwater. Up on deck, a devilish looking machine gun and missiles that can be fired to pinpoint effect. An enormous chair for the captain on the bridge, who appears genial and off-duty, in a voluminous pair of shorts. Down a hatch, along tight little gangways heavy with engine oil, a few sailors squeeze by bound in bath towels. I peer into the confines of an officer's cabin, coveted by the lower ranks sandwiched fifty to a dorm. That evening in the nearby Musée Maritime, a talk is given on the history of Rouen bridges. It seems there was once a moving bridge 'Le Transbordeur', high enough for a plane to fly underneath in the summer of 1912. The aviator named Cavalier.

The impact of the Armada sends ripples of animation across the town. A pack of pompom berets draws applause from the terrace of the 'Café des Fleurs', a formation of imperious peaked caps strides across Place Jeanne d'Arc, and bagpipes shake the walls of Saint Maclou. Rock bands play each night on six squares across the city, and a wonderful clarinetist takes up residence beneath my window on the Rue des Carmes. After ten days of festivity, the Pont Flaubert lowers its drawbridge, rain sweeps across the river and the town turns its back with a customary shrug. For a short passage of time, Rouen 'The Sleeping Giant', whilst not breaking into psychedelic rapture, has emerged smiling from its trance.

***

Travelled up to Leighton Buzzard for an overnight training course. It is a quiet little place with a few Saxon monuments, an empty bus tootling off to Milton Keynes, and people who actually come up and say, 'You're not from round here are you?' At six o'clock the butcher draws a veil over his spread of homemade pies and the High Street goes to sleep. 'The Swan Hotel' has seen better times as a coaching house, alive with merry ale and scrunching carriage wheels. Now it is home to a few builders on bargain basement room rates, ivy invading the windows and corridors imbued with the smell of dead cat. Stepped out for a bite to eat, and discovered a Thai restaurant in a tiny timbered hutch. Excellent grub, but something of a language barrier, all communication conveyed in a frenzy of smiling and bowing, palms held together in a state of servile bliss. The pub down the road filled the void with the footballing giants of Chester City bestriding an enormous screen. Did a final tour of the sights, clambered upto my lumpy bed and awaited the onset of sleep.

The first morning of the course, each participant was asked to respond to the icebreaker – 'Who would you choose to be trapped in a lift with?' Logically the scenario is ridiculous. Given the toxic mix of claustrophobia, escaping wind and a protocol forbidding eye contact, no sane person would want a companion, preferring to plummet the depths

55

of the lift shaft alone. Yet it soon became clear you were meant to select a celebrity chef, and scarily compliant to the corporate culture, everyone offered the required response: "I want to be trapped with Gordon Ramsay because of what he's done for the profession, and because he's such a great bloke." So the supine narrative went on until the Mule chose the human butcher from the film *Delicatessen*. Smitten by his lugubrious face and nimble way with a boning knife.

Delicatessens are the coming thing, every branded coffee shop telling us how they are 'passionate about deli', a sure sign of something dire inside a panini. In Brighton we still have authentic delis. Up on Queens Park Road, Riad serves up original dishes from his native Palestine, something to satisfy every type of vegetarian. On the other side of town, approaching the sea from Sackville Road, 'Coriander' offers a mountain of cheeses, local lamb and exotic cuts of ostrich. David is an enthusiast for real food, interspersing a diatribe against the forces of blandness with a mischievous cackle that could crack open an oyster's shell and make it dance. Sandwiched between these outposts of gastronomy, three fine Bagel Men, offering homemade bagels and infinite fillings. A freshly baked bagel is a live food, the yeast infusing mouth and beak as you break through the crust to reveal the inner life; warm, comforting, salt beef melting over your tongue, sharpened with mustard and pickled gherkin. Once devoured you have no choice. You covet more. Diving down into the depths of the East European 'shtetl', you indulge the next bagel, the tough golden shell yielding into molten chewiness, the impish dance of a violin floating over your head.

***

Down to the Loire to exhibit photos of Brighton Beach. Never broached the borders of Normandy before, so this is new terrain. Gentle hillsides, an abundance of rivers and castles steeped in history. Holed up at the village of Luzillé, 'L'Hôtel du Mail' offering the bare basics of bed, washbasin, and a decor that time forgot. The only other occupants that first night were two women with taut faces, one the finished article, a bent and broken hag. After breakfast a pair of shoes were left outside the toilet, a sure indication of serious business within. Ye gods, after the cistern cranked the corridor filled with a bestial stench, the hanging light bulb fusing before its allotted ten seconds were up. Do French architects compete to design the ultimate airless toilet? Not a window, not a hint of air extraction, just you, four tightly sealed walls and a fulminating bowel action.

The second night my neighbour was a stocky, humpbacked bull of a man, ears and eyes misplaced around his head. The adjoining wall, solid as a net curtain, resounded to his snoring like waves crashing on a stony beach. Evidently this is a hostelry for the local peasant people. After fifty tears under the yoke, pulling udders and sparring with goats, they treat themselves to a night of leisure, requisitioning a bar stool before progressing on to dinner. No need to go reckless, the economy menu would suffice. You could sense the tortuous calculation of what represented best value for money. Pâté or hareng mariné; a demi-carafe or a half bottle of wine? Finally relaxing with a tot of fine Cognac, the hotel must have appeared strangely reassuring. A sparsely peopled bar, barren conversation, a sense of desolation hanging over the place. Nothing to diminish their habitual existence confiding with Daisy in the cowshed.

The next day the exhibition opened in the library of Azay-sur-Indre, a little turret house with thick stone walls and a magical turning staircase. A crowd of about thirty people bustled into the place, speeches were made by doyens of local culture, then everyone cycled off to a neighbouring gallery before returning for lunch. A feast of local endeavour filled a banqueting table in the town hall. Plenty of polite comment about the English 'Cuckmere Valley' wine, and as the alcohol kicked in the afternoon unfolded with a genuine sense of fun. Proceedings culminated with a terrific duo of desserts; savarin steeped in rum and cherry clafoutis, a big fruity Yorkshire pudding. This little corner of French country life included a Chilean who had restored the library, a genial Italian and his Polish wife. It was agreed to open a restaurant with a different cuisine for every month of the year. Overwhelmed by the hospitality and bonhomie, the Mule was sorely tempted.

Some may wonder at a human identifying so closely with a humble beast of burden. But when Jean-Jacques, my host for the night, pointed a torch inside his little stable, I felt confirmed in my identity. A fine figure of an animal with a thick coat and strong legs standing stubborn and proud. And baby mule, muzzle burrowing contentedly into a fresh bundle of hay. When you observe the machinations of humankind, so often turning on gossip and deceit, twisting and scrabbling towards a pinnacle of ambition, then you know that the simple life of a mule is a better place to be.

**

Driving along the front fifteen years ago, Hastings was a depressing place. Facades disintegrating like an ancient mirror reflecting a sepia sea. At periodic intervals word would emerge that Hastings was on the mend, but I always returned to find it empty and dilapidated. Last weekend at the farmers' market, Sue from Carr Taylor vineyard spoke glowingly of the 'Seafood and Wine Festival', so I got on board the stopping train that chugs along Cooden Beach, the odd stray family staring out to sea. A bounding dog caught a ball in its mouth, wove past two defenders, planted the ball in the back of the net and rolled triumphantly on the shingle.

Hastings Station has been transformed into a bright modern campus building. The replica shopping centre is something to be missed, but the Old Town has faded charm and an original line in boutiques. Meandered through a mazy bookshop, finding myself in the owners' kitchen, and wandered back to discover a three-year-old in charge of the till. The window of 'Butlers Famed Emporium' displayed every household accessory from a time when housewives wore headscarves, gingham pinnies and brown stockings. A balloon floated past, bravely proclaiming 'I Love Hastings.'

On the beach, the lifeboat house was filled with a choir, announcing the Festival in full swing. A fine array of local drinks on display: 'Saxon Valley' wine, Carr Taylor bubbly, and a scorchingly dry Battle cider that shook the palette and left it spinning. Every style of fish cuisine billowed into the sky, and an enormous queue waited patiently for two local fillets fried in a bun; all for just two pounds. I settled for a tapas platter of marinated herring, smoked pâté on crunchy bread, and an intensely roasted tomato worthy of the name 'love apple.' Found a hollow on the pebbles to enjoy my meal with a glass of Biddenden wine. Sheltered by a line of steeply pitched fishermen's huts, from where Mother Seagull surveyed her swarm of chicks. At the end of the Prom, a magnificent building rose like an ocean liner, sparkling in the autumn sun.

I watched the little funicular carriage as it climbed the precipitous cliff. History would have been different had King Harold commanded those heights when the Vikings stormed the beach, a ready supply of boiling oil dispatching them back to Normandy. As it was, the armies met in a field five miles north of Hastings, in a place that curiously retains the name of Battle. Arrived there by train, and the station was an unexpected surprise; solid stone walls, ecclesiastical windows and a glowing fire in the ticket office. On the walk up to town, every sign pointed to a bellicose past. 'Powder Mill Lane' leading to the gunpowder works that lit up the Napoleonic Wars. And a hundred takes on 1066. The High Street was filled with taverns, tea rooms and original little shops. 'Ye Olde Battle Axe', a second-hand clothes store with a redoubtable matron in charge, 'Yesterday's World' offering a guide to the past, and 'The Almony', an exquisite building dispensing civic advice. Behind it, a public garden with the perfect potting shed; gingerbread shutters beside lattice windows and curly red tiles on top. Benches lined the flower beds, dedicated to fallen Battle folk.

The main attraction was the Abbey, its grounds bordering the field where the Anglo Saxon army succumbed in a single day. It was built in reparation for the carnage wrought in battle, and some of the monuments have been faithfully restored. Great stone barns that housed valued guests, an impressive line of latrines and a cavernous building running down the hillside that was home to novice monks. Lights out, eyes down, and the ancient ritual of 'bashing the bishop' took hold. A proud tradition doubtless maintained in the boarding school that now occupies much of the Abbey.

The journey home required a change of train at St. Leonards Warrior Square and I strolled along, idling time away. A cafe-cum-bakery with a smoked glass partition secluding the seated guests. Iced buns with glacé cherries, Battenburg and Eccles cakes. A little artwork shop, a greengrocer and two butchers. The most contemporary sign was 'Rumanian Appeal' banded across the window of a charity shop. Ceausescu disappeared over twenty years ago, but when your town assumes the profile of warriors past, expect to be trapped in a time warp.

***

All the turkey dinners are captive inside a convoy of oven trolleys, steaming away in a banqueting room at the

Metropole Hotel. The magnificent vaulted ceiling filled with the smell of stuffing and the golden light of chandeliers. An empty stretch of time prior to the guests arriving, the army of waiting staff from a hundred different lands, yawning and chatting quietly. Marshalled into shape by Zelda, a magnificent West Indian woman who whoops and gasps, recounting the scene from last night when a couple were discovered at it like rabbits; rabbits in stilettos, top hat and tails. She is interrupted with a question about gluten-free diets, and we launch into an impromptu take on the Simon and Garfunkel song: 'Oh Ceciliac, you're breaking my heart.'

Two chefs; me and a cold German who certainly doesn't sing, but takes an intense relish in snapping his towel whenever a sleepy waiter parks his butt on the table. Just two chefs and two porters, ready to unload the turkey wagons, fatigue becoming a factor in the absence of something to do. I shift my weight from one hot hoof to the other, and listen to the porter from Uzbekistan describing the treasured place of horse meat in his national cuisine. Every part of the animal savoured, none more so than – you guessed it – the testicles. Then the gun fires and we are off, red hot cloches cast aside, bone-dry meat sauced and the raggle taggle brigade of waiters marching into the dining hall where five hundred call centre workers are attending their Xmas 'do.' All in their finery and tinselled plumage, relishing the transient sense of social climbing, and just on the brink of tipping from Sunday best to rip roaring raucous.

Up until ten years ago, a flotilla of centurion waitresses would have carried enormous platters into the banqueting arena, proudly manipulating fork and spoon like castanets, deftly plating the paraphernalia of chipolata, stuffing and sprouts in a seamless round of silver service. The modern brigade are cut adrift from these old waiting skills, and have an original approach to customer care. Waitresses greet the guests with smiles like chinks in the Iron Curtain; young lads wired together, nodding away to an iPod. Deficiencies concealed by smart white tunics, gleaming brass buttons, sleeves impeccably pressed.

Preparations at home for the yuletide feast turn a little sluggish. First an athletic nocturnal cough, then all energy sapping away, like a cold sea mist rolling in and taking control. All engagements annulled, curtains drawn and the Mulehouse plunged into a sorry torpor. Four muzzles wrapped in muslin steeped in Olbas oil, breakfast oats left untouched, coats bereft of sheen, tails still and unbrushed. Gradually the cloud lifts, and I try a shift at The Metropole, the whole hotel booked for a week by Roche the pharmaceutical giant. The next time you hear a silken voice explain how all profits are spent on research and development, think of a free, bounteous bonanza beside the sea, the Prince Regent Room transformed into Brighton beach with a merry-go-round, shooting gallery and coconut shies. Meanwhile in the subterranean kitchens, the nearest you get to a breath of briny is the fetid gale of dustbin stench howling up the back passage. There must have been a deluge in the outside world, because rain is rising up through the drains, and work on the dinner ensues with water lapping about your feet. Then six little Sri Lankans arrive, wide-eyed and naive, and they are set to work putting nine hundred burgers into nine hundred sesame seed buns.

One particularly stubborn tray unhinges the old back, and I march doggedly up Elm Grove for a physio appointment in the workhouse. The temperature inside hovers around 40°c, the perfect incubator for germ warfare. A brisk young girl examines the poor old vertebrae, bend this way, then that, and now lie back. Had I got a sensation like trapped wind? Confidently reply that I'd never been party to such a complaint, and as if on cue, fire one off with a flourish that flutters the curtains. The temperature rises another notch, Mademoiselle bristles, her pony tail twitching, clearly uncomfortable with the animal habits of a rogue Brighton male. But I love her and follow her exercises morning and night, determined to be fit to pound the turf and gallop around the racecourse.

Successive arctic winters, and the carefree dress sense that assumed olive groves on The Downs has disappeared. Scour the town in deepest January and you will not find a single pair of baggy trousers cut off at the knee. We're all battened down in tundra gear – hoods, ear mufflers and industrial long johns. During a brief thaw, the queue for unclaimed mail outside the Post Office in North Road straggles halfway up the hill. Two plodding posties man the office at a sedentary pace, and there is precious little movement as the wind whips along the street. The queue frozen in stoical silence, no communication about power cuts or ration cards, just a lone plaintive cry from an orphan that's lost its mitten. Outside the depot, the waste bin contains meticulous instructions for use.

'Stubber' to indicate spent cigarettes, and unmistakably embossed on the opposite side, three brazen letters spelling 'Cum'. Quite nonplussed at the notion of arousal in an icy wind tunnel, but I am cold beyond caring and rational thought. Austerity times have diminished all sense of feeling. I finally shuffle into the shelter of the vestibule, and approach the counter to claim my parcel of coal, a Xmas gift from Silesia dispatched 'Special Delivery'.

***

I have tried to find an affinity with seagulls, but it is a seriously hard task. Avoiding all eye contact and social chit chat, they just sit aloft smoking Woodbines, farting like cannons and scratching their tits. No respect for the convention of silence before dawn, their raucous cries saw through the night, shredding all prospect of sleep. The pigeons aren't much better. They've got a favourite tree in the Pavilion Gardens, commanding the bare winter branches like cold grey battle axes. They've seen it all before of course, the Prince Regent tunnelling into Mrs Fitzherbert's and the students tumbling out. Not the slightest effort to summon a gentle cooing, or a tremulous Piaf lament, just intent on targeting tourists with white plutonium pigeon crap.

So I was intrigued today by the sight of two gulls dancing on the spot, webbed feet beating out time like a demented vaudeville act. The shock of seagulls actually doing something, the wonderment of why and the fact that the two birds actually seemed to connect. No overt display of petting and pecking, but fond looks and casual patter passed between their beaks. Perhaps they'd enrolled at Hanover community centre for a course in finding the inner self. Or strictly avian tap dance. Or the bin bags outside the Ocean Rooms were peppered with sparkling magic dust.

Further along The Level, another gull was stomping away as if his life depended on it. I had to discount the intense February cold as a cause, as seagulls never seem happier than bobbing about on glacial waters without so much as a pair of gloves. Carried on to the Brighthelm Centre for a performance of Jewish and Russian songs. What an infinite source of grief. On the one side, centuries of serfdom, black bread, the slaughter of the kulaks and Stalingrad. On the other, the presumption that the world turns on a treadmill of shrugs. As a child growing up in the ghetto of North West London, I could never understand how the Jewish concept of festival or holiday had nothing to do with fun. Great numbers would gather to 'celebrate' the holy days, too many to be contained in the normal synagogue, so the cinema was requisitioned for the purpose. Curtain up and lights down on a performance of slow, doleful incantation where time slipped into reverse gear. Just twice during the New Year and Harvest festivals excitement smouldered around the blowing of the 'shofar.' Now getting music out of a ram's horn was no easy task. Mr. Baum who taught the backward class at my primary school, huffed and puffed to absolutely no effect. Cue scuffling exit with that trademark squeaking boot. Enter Jerome, a big powerful man, his prayer shawl clothing a colossal set of lungs. A few preliminary manoeuvres to garner anticipation and rid the horn of spit, then he was off on a succession of rich stentorian sounds culminating in one long breath-defying note. It was like a call to arms and the cinema rose to its feet. 'Shakoyach!', the Yiddish equivalent of 'Go on my son', rippled through the auditorium. Outside, a line of pigeons pattered their feet on the tiles and practiced protracted cooing.

***

You could base your stay in Rouen within sight of the cathedral walls. I have booked into every hostelry thereabouts, and no matter how threadbare the carpet or rubberized the under-sheet, so long as the room is at the top of a turning staircase, you will open your window onto that magnificent view. The spire rising protectively over its three little chick spires, one famously lost in the hurricane of 1999. The bells in 'Le Tour de Beurre' peeling away haphazardly, conjuring images of cassocks flailing in mid air. Lines of imperious bishops on the ridges of the West wall, looking down contemptuously on the crowd below, dark eyes summoning fear. Beware men wearing robes.

Nothing can surpass the Hotel Cardinal, with a bird's eye view of 'Le Parvis', the cobbled cathedral square. Warm welcome, excellent breakfast, and two stout restaurants on either side. 'Chez Alain' serves up enormous meaty salads with duck breast, chicken livers and gizzards. Trade is so good, they can afford to shut at weekends. Next door, 'Café Paul' offers a traditional Norman menu and a Maître D orchestrating proceedings with absolute economy of movement; an undemonstrative raised finger, a nod of recognition, a satisfied tug on the cuffs. Scott Joplin music tinkles away on one of those automatic pianos that really needs to learn a longer repertoire. Tonight I take up residence in the window seat, watching the cathedral stones glow in the evening sun, soften in shadow and withdraw into night. A million starlings burst into life in a salvo of song and missiles; judicious to avoid the path beneath the plane trees during evening chorus. The birds eventually settle down to sleep, wisely ignoring the 'son et lumière' show which this year throws up a shapeless jumble of colours on the cathedral walls, accompanied by arid jarring music.

Far better to make for 'Le Musée des Beaux Arts', where a memorable performance unfolds. This is a majestic two storey building, with great lines of windows that act as the frames for Impressionist canvases. Familiar images swirl across the facade, like a merry-go-round in your mind. The picnic party on the river bank, the Renoir dancers, the giant steam engine breathing fire in the Gare du Nord. The whole building transforms into a riot of dappled colours, then the focus becomes more precise, revealing the detail of brushwork, the Van Gogh old man with crop circle eyes. Each visual impression has an accompanying soundtrack; rain streaming down the walls and coursing through the drains, the bellowing of a tricolour crowd on the Fourteenth of July. And so much is open to interpretation; waves curling high on the tide, or are they stars spinning in the sky? I left wanting more and returned for three successive nights, each one filled with delight.

***

Festival time sketches a new dimension onto our everyday lives. An intimate audience with the absurd inside an antique Volks railway carriage. Set up on a picket fenced lawn outside the Jubilee library, a butler bearing a curious resemblance to Lenin dispenses free gin & tonics. Perhaps the sealed train that spirited Lenin to Russia in 1917 was in fact a Volks carriage. Vladimir Ilyich, Zinoviev and Kamenev sitting opposite each other in a little wooden compartment, raising their hands cheerfully at passersby. No room for Stalin though, that smelly peasant could not afford the fare from the Aquarium to Black Rock, let alone Zurich to Petrograd. Little did they realise how deeply he would harbour a grudge.

Court Farm artists' collective sits at the top of Dyke Road, with a powerful view of the sea. Totem poles and wind-driven wigwams stake out the grass, the farm building exhibiting everything from haute couture to mosaic glass. There's a tangible sense of freedom in the air, people going about their collective tasks with a lightness and creative purpose. Something akin to the vibe surrounding 'No Fit State Circus' which set up camp on The Level last weekend. A great name really, eschewing any sense of expectation. If the mono cyclist gets a puncture and the trapeze act freezes with vertigo, you won't be disappointed. In truth there was little memorable about the performance beyond carnival drumming, a burlesque band and two husky bellows breathing red smoke. The audience really made the show, generous and exuberant.

'Chouf Ouchouf', a Moroccan acrobat troupe, took the Corn Exchange by storm. They began like a motley bunch of joggers gone to seed, lazily limbering up in baggy tracksuits, one man chugging around the stage with sun visor and plastic water bottle. At an invisible sign the audience hushed and the performers effortlessly mounted a human scaffold three stories high, then dissembled into a choreography of snappy summersaults, catherine wheels driven on by a North African beat. Impossible to maintain this tempo indefinitely, the cast leaned against a backdrop of blank urban concrete, chewing and staring languidly, until the wall suddenly came to life, propelling the Moroccans forward in a gathering commotion of disbelief. Stopping just short of the orchestra pit, the wall broke into four separate towers, each deftly coasting about the stage, swallowing and disgorging performers like a magical conjuring box. A current of humour passed through the auditorium; the circus gasp as an acrobat toppled backwards into oblivion. A bright red fez perched on a lugubrious face, reappearing suspended without a head. Tommy Cooper's trademark titfer. You could extract interpretations with the 'Arab Spring', but the impact was pure entertainment.

**

Filed into Saint Bartholomew's for a performance of Mahler's Fifth. The buzz of anticipation muted by the righteous hush and cold comfort of an English church. The players of the Sussex Symphony Orchestra took to the stage in traditional penguin wear, followed by the conductor in a black silk number, deftly cut to accommodate the fuller figure. Never before has Mahler been interpreted by a man in a shiny kimono. The towering brick walls gave the sound a rougher edge, and the horns ripped through the roof with uproarious dissent. Grief, euphoria, an immense wave of sound retreating on a tide of violins. The principal bassoon launched into a solo, lips tightly folded around the reed like the wiggle of the Loch Ness monster. Number Two bassoon sat motionless beside her, the same tension taut across her face. The most distant double bass player appeared lost in distress. Sombre eyes glowering in their orbits, solid Victorian sideburns like bookends of distaste. The conductor was the fulcrum of the piece, beating and coaxing, red neck straining, kimono glistening with sweat. A truly bravura performance.

Further down the London Road, the star turn of the Festival extended way into the summer. An old man teetering on the edge of life was the focal point of 'And So To Sleep.' A dreamy piece of performance art set in the cavernous basement and faded splendour of the disused Co-op department store. An old waiter, no longer able to remember the names of customers he has served for generations, opened proceedings in nightshirt and long johns, his weary face sculpted by the yellow flame of a candle. He later emerged confused and adrift in the bedding department of the old store, and was unceremoniously ushered away. Images of his figure in stiff collar and black tails appeared throughout the set. Wandering through a block of flats, a maze of trees, an enormous dolls house where children might escape the trauma of family life.

Each visitor experienced a unique voyage of discovery. A dim light through darkness leading to a glowing winter landscape. Teacups, birdsong and bristling bourgeois disaffection. A redundant stockroom like a requiem for lost mannequins. The enduring sequence was of the old man laying down in a wood, confused and babbling, the camera turning slowly through a kaleidoscope of trees, then rising to reveal the shores of a desert island. Life ending desolate as an abandoned department store, a certain dignity of purpose not to be found again.

***

Sitting at a café terrace in Dieppe, the lady of the house appeared for her public at the end of the Rue de la Barre. She greeted the couple at the neighbouring table with an accomplished, 'Bonjour monsieur / dame', but then did a double take realising the 'male' figure was in fact a lesbian. 'Oh je m'excuse, bonjour mesdames, mes dames! The light does play tricks at times.' Sad to see this indomitable lady reduced to mumbling ineptitude. The offended party hurrumphed and stirred restlessly in her seat, then pulled up a sleeve to reveal a limb hairier than a bear. The lesbian was indeed a man. With that Madame gave up on the whole affair and went back indoors; cucumber slices over her eyes and intravenous Pernod.

Pondered this incident as I sat at a restaurant terrace in Rouen. This is all I do in France, imbibe excellent food and drink, scribble down the odd phrase and retire for a siesta. Normans are notoriously reluctant to spend their cash, but occasionally push the boat out for dinner in a decent restaurant. Apéritifs savoured, a bottle of Château wine uncorked and then the serious business of tackling a plate of bloody meat. A huge rib of beef was presented to the next door table, returned to the kitchen for the briefest flirtation with a flame, and finally carved at a gueridon trolley. The full carnivore ceremonial. The three guests watched the whole display, smoking intently. A silent couple and a stocky older man who bore all the hallmarks of 'Le Normand Costaud.' Solid fusion of trunk and neck, rolls of chin and eyes devoid of merriment.

My main course was a rich meaty number, containing a delicacy found inside the pig's ear. Did not go a bundle on this, unable to banish the concept of ear wax, but both potato purée and bread were excellent. Not the shameful stick of cotton wool typical of an English baguette, but a crunchy, chewy, nutty crust that yielded the scent of wood smoke. Just enough wispiness inside to mop up any remaining sauce, the dishwasher made redundant.

Après-kip, took a cycle ride beside the little River Robec that tinkles along between the hills of La Grande Mare and Mont Gargnan. Once alive with threshing water wheels, grinding wheat and spinning cloth, the mills fell into neglect towards the end of the last century. Some have recently been restored, and one vast brick mill that wove cotton and rubber into braces, is now the school of architecture. The only concession to modernism are two bright spiral staircases with catwalks leading into the building, the ironwork draped with students lapping up the sunshine. That evening, the sky across the Channel had an architecture all of its own. Dark banks of cloud sealing Dieppe into the night, clean bright clouds overhead and a soft orange sunset capturing the silhouette of a ship on the horizon. Two ends of a rainbow stood up through the darkness like fluorescent sticks of rock. An arc was formed, faint at the apex but all the more magnificent for the delicate effect. Then drained of all energy, the rainbow did that Monet thing and melted into the sky.

The following morning, climbed the hill to Newhaven Fort, clumps of pretty mauve flowers sunning themselves on the cliffs, the slim barrel of a plucky little cannon defying Bonaparte and the Boche. Through a long tunnel into a reconstruction of Britain at war. Calls to conscription, air raid sirens and shelters shaken by bombs. The night in 1944 when a barge loaded with high explosive, broke loose in high seas, collided with a mine in the harbour and lifted the people of Newhaven clean out of their beds. The young pilot who shot down a V1 missile and died in the ensuing blast, and a graphic account of the 1942 attack on Dieppe. More than one hundred RAF planes were lost in a single day, and thousands of soldiers slaughtered beneath the sheer Normandy cliffs.

One survivor recollected walking over corpses and body parts as the Germans indulged in a clay pigeon shoot. A Canadian reunited back in Sussex with just two remnants of his entire regiment. The whole insane mission a gesture to Stalin that an attempt had been made to open a Western Front. Two years later a Sussex schoolboy enlisted on a vessel supporting 'Operation Overlord.' It must have been strange returning to his wooden desk, with an inky pen and a logarithm book.

***

White waves rolling high above The Downs, preceded by dark fluffy clouds suspended like inky thumbprints. The train draws in with a passenger snoring thunderously. Welcome to Eastbourne. Here to visit the Towner Gallery that has drawn rave reviews for its modern architecture. From the second floor balcony, you look out onto the green baize of tennis courts, scorched brown in patches by pristine white footwear. The solid brick turret of an affluent private school rises against a background of verdant hills. Walk back towards town, past 'Serenity', a magnificent funeral emporium, and a gaggle of trundling shopping trolleys, briefly disturbed by a delinquent turbo-charged wheelchair. I worked here at the university for seven years, and only recall a single memorable place. The little café inside the station run by Terry and Robert. They came from a theatrical background and every morning was a little performance as complete strangers gesticulated on their stools, dispensed banter, and dunked their croissants with a final flourish before heading off for the train. I cycled up the hill to the campus at Meads Village, discreet and undemonstrative as Miss Marple's raised eyebrow. Eastbourne, safe and unspectacular, stillness impregnating the air, the horizon petering out into a fusion of sea and sky.

And now it has been outdone by Brighton in the bandstand stakes. For decades the Brighton edifice stood dilapidated, then hidden from view as lengthy restoration took place. Suddenly the scaffolding disappeared to reveal a jewel of intricate ironwork, an exquisite sculpture perched above the Prom. This weekend, 'Chutzpah', a Jewish ladies' choir took up residence. Their leader swept about ostentatiously in a long red housecoat, eventually discarded to reveal a scarlet velvet number that hugged her body in all the right places. I remember housecoats from my childhood – Jewish women were born in them. But a voluptuous woman without sideburns, that was something new. Every chant of the chorus was a variation on 'Oihh', delivered with such verve that the massed ranks of deckchairs were roused from their sun-baked stupor. One man who minutes before resembled a stricken monkfish, prone and gasping for breath, now leapt to his pins and beat his hands together with electric vigour. Heads were nodding, faces smiling, sticks stomping, and not a knotted white handkerchief in sight.

**

A walk down Upper North Street unearths original images of Brighton life. Old time tailors with dummies and scrolls of measuring tape. The legendary cuisine of 'Barry at The Tureen.' A glass display case in the window of number 44, carrying a description of the scene within:

'Father floated downstream on a kitchen table.

I accompanied on the piano as the water rose.'

And indeed, one figure is perched on an upturned table, the other on an Oxford piano, both adrift on a rushing tide of blue. However, neither bear any resemblance to a human being, but a remarkable creature with bird-like head, rodent body and reptilian shell. The bastard child of an estate agent. A second glass case depicts a story to the legend 'The butcher's fear of the carcass.' A fresh cast surveys a chicken splayed on the chopping block, with the butcher looking on mortified. His fish face stricken with a sense of terror, like a sea bream caught in the hold of a boat, frozen in an alien environment.

At the end of the street is Saint Nicholas' Church which dates back to 1091, when John of Brighthelmstone presided over the pulpit. The graveyard contains several noteworthy residents. Captain Tattersall who spirited Charles II across the sea. Martha Gunn the famous bather. And Phoebe Hessel who disguised herself as a man to join the infantry and was wounded at the battle of Fontenoy. At eighty seven she was still selling apples and gingerbread on the Old Steine, lived to witness the coronation of the Prince Regent and finally keeled over at the sterling age of one hundred and eight. At 'The Cook & Fiddle' we had a great old customer who walked down to the beach each day from nearby Clifton Terrace, his slight frame defying the wind to blow him clean away. Impeccably attired in jacket and tie, he would settle down inside the arch to a pot of tea and a scone. However strong you made the brew, he always added an extra tea bag from his pocket, and recounted plans to celebrate his ninetieth birthday the following February. Well the next season came around with no sign of our old friend, presumably preserved in St. Nicholas' churchyard by a lifelong intake of tannin.

An historic insight into valiant survival recently opened at the Royal Pavilion. A room devoted to the time when the Pavilion was given over to Indian soldiers wounded in the First World War. There is a motion picture of turbaned invalids relaxing in the grounds. The Dome transformed into a huge circular ward, dignified faces emerging from starched white sheets. One bedazzled soldier, Subedar-Major Sardar Bahadur Gurgan, expressed his wonderment at the place.

'Everything is such as one would not see even in a dream.
One should regard it as fairyland.
The heart cannot be satiated with seeing the sights,
for there is no other place like this in the world.
It is as if one were in the next world... I have never been
so happy in my life as I am here.'

***

Amble up to the counter at 'The Red Roaster', milk building up a head of steam, cups stacked, beans ground and dispensed, clickety clack, into the mighty coffee machine that stands like a monument to roasted Arabica. Exchange football talk with Simone, the pearl of a manageress, survey the scene for a table far from 'Infinity' mum and her suckling offspring, and settle, infusing beak in cup, perusing the paper, back to the cup, and for a time there is nothing beyond carefree capers in a bubble bath, that could possibly improve my life. A writer drifts off into the cloud of inspiration floating above his Apple Mac. A queen sips and simpers, averting his probing eye, like an imperious parrot on a perch. And a boy with blond curls, radiates cheeky confidence beneath a baggy blue cap; parents' faces drooping, drained by the little powerhouse they produced too late in life. The white 'crema' breaks into flotsam, streaking the sides of the coffee cup, like a spent tide retreating on the beach. A strident French voice begins to invade my space, and someone breaks out of the disabled toilet revealing a scene of distress. The aura of contentment has passed.

A Turkish café has just opened on the Lewes Road. All day, a woman sits at a low table in the window, headscarf tied, apron struggling to contain a formidable bosom. She commands a long thin rolling pin, coaxing tangerine-sized balls of dough into pancakes, filling them with spinach and potato, then turning them on a griddle proud as a kettle drum. Golden brown, this is the most wonderful fast food, light crisp and only two pounds a time. The room out the back is all cushions, low tables and candle light. Coyness left behind at the pub, a group of locals breaks into an original form of belly dancing; the hanging bellies of Bevendean. Tev at the

Turkish Food Market tells me that an Ottoman restaurant is soon to appear, equipped with the same charcoal grill that imbues lamb with aromatic scorchiness at 'Cirric' on White Hart Lane. Things are on the up.

Cycling home, I catch sight of a short square man with a large jaw, cradling his dog in his arms like a giant glove muffler. He climbs the steps to his house, an intense expression imprinted on his face, something between delight and distress. Neither dog nor owner look well. Indeed the dog may already be dead, but the man just cannot accept that Mutley will never again be a contender in the quadruped lamppost stakes.

***

For thirty years a terrible concrete building imposed on the majesty of the cathedral square. 'Le Palais du Congres' was so brutally ugly, the connecting passageway so steeped in tramp's piss, that no human being could contemplate working there, and it stood empty and decayed, a cold and barren presence intruding on the Gothic splendour of old Rouen. This week two steel pterodactyls began the work of destruction. Tenacious teeth nibbling relentlessly at the belly of the beast to reveal a bleak interior, cables hanging from the ceilings shrouded with brick dust, swaying gently in the wind like a host of hangman's nooses. Logically the new space should be left calm and unfettered, a little oasis to reflect the splendour of the soaring cathedral walls. Such is the power of real estate that another building is already planned, but surely nothing can equal the barbarity of the previous structure. Will have to get Prince Charles on the case.

Off to Dieppe today to dine with Manu Concombre. Manu is that rare thing, a smiling Norman, with the sweeping coat and sparkling eye of a gigolo. We arranged to have lunch at 'Tout Va Bien', a seafood restaurant in Dieppe. Took the little train that meanders beside the dancing brook that is the River Scie. An exaggerated stop at Auffay presaged something untoward, and after a few juddering starts the engine ground to a halt at the timbered village of Longueville-sur-Scie. The residents were blockading the line, protesting at a cut in the number of stopping trains each day. Pitch forks brandished at the window, Robespierre climbed aboard and requisitioned the intercom: 'Mesdames, messieurs, camarades…' Leaflets were circulated and in true French style every passenger swore solidarity with the cause, vowed to remonstrate with SNCF and sang *The International*. Suitably satisfied, the train was allowed to carry on to Dieppe, and I cycled off for lunch.

Manu Concombre has the wonderful habit of sending back a bottle of wine, no explanation required, the imperious nature of the request dispatching the waiter like a squirrel down a hole. Today he found no fault and I settled down to a plate of scallops with a fine Sancerre wine. A stocky couple inhabited the neighbouring table, he with jowls working furiously, she solid and built to last, hair held back in an iron clasp. Traditionally in these parts, the arrival of the bill would occasion forensic examination, every item from apéritif to digestif subjected to close scrutiny. But today the amount was paid with barely a second glance, and even a few centimes were tossed into the saucer before departing. Maupassant and Flaubert mercilessly painted these people as mean and miserly; something which struck a chord with the Mule when resident of Rouen. Now, strange to tell, there are unprecedented signs of expansiveness.

Stranger still, nocturnal animation as rock bands shook the bejesus out of the ancient cathedral walls. Setting up camp in a Big Top beside the South gate, the music throbbed through my bedroom in the Hotel Cardinal. Every now and again the plug was pulled, the acclaim of the crowd subsided, and I laid in hope of nothing more intrusive than a bell summoning old ladies to prayer. Then a fresh Techno salvo ripped through the night, and a tortured state of insomnia was assured. These days, the nearest I get to something loud and wired is the journey inside the body scanner at the Royal Sussex County. All self-respect stripped away as the pale blue nightdress splays wide open just when a neighbour unaccountably walks into the room. The camp attendant rolls you into the lunar module, where you are assailed by an electronic sound storm reminiscent of Club Shame twenty years ago. Seriously honed bodies performed hedonistic rituals on three giant hat boxes that stood proud of the crowd. There was one lean boy whose body mirrored the music like a wave. Bare topped, ethereal smile; I wonder what became of him? Hips probably giving him jip as the scanner gets ready to roll.

***

Peered over the seafront balustrade at one of those café billboards serving every variation of saturated fat. Ripples scuffed the surface of a lazy sea, the groynes lurking in the shallows like submarines. A flotilla of leather bikers coasted up to the beach on a wall of sound. Two men in monocles and bowler hats cycled by on penny farthings. Sydney Seagull turned his head and tutted, singularly unimpressed.

Further along the Prom a film set was in full swing for a re-make of *Brighton Rock*. They recreated a picture of early 1960's England. Beach hut furniture adorned with Melamine plates, knitting wool and a 'Bush' transistor radio. Carefree girls with candy floss hair and fly away skirts; older women battening down expectations of fun with tightly knotted headscarfs. Two boys in shorts and bedraggled socks, ran up to an ice cream van selling 'Zoom' lollies for nine old pence. John Hurt sauntered by with that smooth yet gravelly diction. Dame Helen, framed in the murky window of a beach shelter, remonstrated with the profile of a villain. Then the new 'Pinky' took centre stage. Once saw him play a terrific role as Ian Curtis, lead singer of 'Joy Division'; here he was a cocky Mod with scarred cheekbone and a Spitfire logo on his Parka.

Sydney soared through the sultry air, and cast a Republican shadow over the statue of Queen Victoria. Glided over the Pavilion Gardens where a man on stilts played the tuba with insouciant grace. Followed the Lewes Road, over the Peoples' Park, where sunflowers wound their way up the wire fencing and tilted their faces towards the sky. Oblivious to the motorists fermenting inside their throbbing cells. Sydney carried on to Falmer, and pondered the acquisition of a season ticket on the floodlight at the Polytechnic End. For a guaranteed place, and his name inscribed on a concrete plinth, he paid an annual levy of two hundred herring to the Chairman in the Executive box. But it was worth it. Even for a tight-beaked, weary old bird such as he, it did the soul good to hear the Seagulls roar. And if things turned pear-shaped on the pitch, he knew how to direct his displeasure at Mister Cigar Face in the herringbone suit.

***

Chapter 2

Black & White photographs of Sussex and Upper Normandy

Brighton Beach

Palace Pier

Launching the Wheel

Building the Wheel

Thomas

Penny Farthing

Sea Horse

Old Ship Clowns

'Brighton Rock' Film Set

Volks Railway

Sand Sculptures

Surfing Santas

Images of Brighton

Royal Pavilion

Pavilion Café

Lenin in Jubilee Square

St Peter's Owl

Red Roaster Café

Café Motu

Phoenix Gallery

Colonnade Bar

North Laine Flamingos

Strange Fruit

Falmer Stadium

Parking on 'The Level'

Snow Pigeon

Bikes in the snow

Writing on the wall

Lewes Road

Trees Replaced Cars…

Sydney Street

Pelham Square

Message on High

Nest Egg

Into Sussex

Southwick Sea Road

Shoreham

Lewes

Breaky Bottom Vineyard

Launch of Seafood Festival

South Downs Lamb

Offham Farm Pig

To Dieppe

Newhaven Fort

Transmanche Ferry

Scallop Boat

Dieppe Docks

The Harbour

Dieppe Beach

Dieppe Castle

Rouen and Beyond

Rue du Gros Horloge

Rouen Cathédrale

Charcuterie

School of Architecture

Building the Pont Flaubert

Rouen Docks

Rouen Armada

The Armada

Clair de Lune

Norman Cottage

Norman at Home

Parc de Clères

Goat Farm Bellencombre

Bellencombre

Chartres

Chapter 3

The Mule Guide to Real Food in Sussex

The last decade has seen a renaissance in food and drink from Sussex. Our wines win awards in Paris, rare breeds are restored to The Downs and new cheeses spring up like magic mushrooms. The list of quality local producers expands with every week, so The Mule Guide confines itself to first hand experience; tasting the fodder, quaffing the drink or setting hoof on the farm.

Dairy

<u>High Weald Dairy</u> organic cheeses. Mark and Sarah Hardy have been producing prize-winning cheeses for over 20 years in the Ashdown Forest, home of Pooh Bear. They used to inhabit an idyllic thatched farm in Duddleswell, but such has been their success they have moved to larger premises at Horsted Keynes.

They offer a wide variety of sheep cheeses. The hard and nutty Duddleswell, feta, halloumi and Sussex Slipcote; this last one comes as a creamy log, rolled in peppercorns or herbs & garlic.

Then there are cheeses made from cows' milk. Tremains cheddar, Ashdown Forester and Saint Giles which is similar to Port Salut. A new arrival is Organic Soster which resembles parmesan. Much farm produce suffers from being inaccessible, but the High Weald Dairy has long been ahead of the game, delivering weekly to shops and caterers.

☎ 01825 791636 ☛info@highwealddairy.co.uk

Nut Knowle goat cheese. A few years ago, cycling up the 'Cuckoo Trail' I tried to find Nut Knowle Farm but circled Horam to no avail. An internet search led to a primitive website with the bald choice, click on 'Goat Farm' or 'Goat Sperm.' I did neither and let the whole Nut Knowle venture lie. Now you can't get away from them, their cheese is on show at every farmers market in every form, rolled in ash, shaped into pyramids, steeped in olive oil

☎ 01825 872214 ☛jj@nutknowlefarm.com

Golden Cross make two distinctive cheeses on their farm near Lewes. 'Golden Cross' is made from goats' milk, and the sumptuous 'Flower Marie' from sheep. Sometimes elusive, they can usually be found at 'Cheese Please', Fiona's abundant little shop on Lewes High Street.

☎ 01825 872380 ☛kevinblunt@btconnect.com

<u>Sussex Blue and Sussex Brie</u> are two excellent cheeses produced at Five Ashes.

First encountered at a wine and cheese tasting hosted by Christopher Ann at The English Wine Centre. Sadly, Christopher is no longer at the helm as his knowledge of food and wine was unsurpassed.

☎ 01825 831810 ☞bestbier@btinternet.com

<u>Plaw Hatch biodynamic cheese & yoghurt</u>. Biodynamic seems quite a technical term, but it in fact relates to a form of agriculture that existed widely before intensive farming. Plaw Hatch is a mixed farm of horned cattle and organic fruit & vegetables. It is self-contained, using its own seeds for planting, and feeding cattle from crops grown on the farm. The rhythm of the moon & planets is important in deciding when to sow and harvest.

Unpasteurised milk is used to prevent loss of B vitamins and beneficial bacteria. The farm is a Co-operative which keeps the prices low when you consider the quality of their vintage cheddar. They also produce an original range of fruit yoghurts.

☎ 01342 810201 ☞ farmCo-op@hotmail.co.uk

<u>Bookhams cheese & butter</u>. The 'Sussex Charmer' is a neatly packaged cheese, a fusion of cheddar and parmesan. Butter comes in attractive rounds, both salted and unsalted.

☎ 01323 636110 ☞ info@bookhams.com

Downsview Farm ice cream, milk & thick cream. I first met the Downsview folk at a book event in Worthing that promoted Sussex produce. Their honeycomb ice cream was simply stunning, and the double cream a match for any scone. They also do a big range of sorbets. Regular deliveries throughout the region.

☎ 01825 841002 ☞ info@downsviewfarm.co.uk

Willetts Farm ice cream. Before opening 'The Cook & Fiddle' I intended to make ice cream, as it seemed essential for a seafront location. However, the narrow kitchen in the old Arch left no space for a commercial machine. So I bought Willetts Farm ices, excellent vanilla and chocolate as well as peach yoghurt. They now do 16 flavours and deliver weekly.

☎ 01892 740320 ☞ robin@willettsfarm.co.uk

Meat, poultry and game

There has been a terrific growth in the number of farms rearing quality livestock in Sussex, some organically raised, others promoting rare breeds.

Oaks Poultry Farm. When chef lecturer at City College I took a coach load of students for a tour of the Ridgeview wine estate, just north of Ditchling. On the way home we stopped to buy poultry from nearby Oaks Farm, and prepared it for the college restaurant that evening. Chicken liver pâté with apple and cinnamon; herby lemon chicken with potato rosti; medlar fruit ice cream and sparkling Ridgeview wine. We had a good old tour of the barns, and it was great to have the experience of sourcing a dinner direct from the farm.

☎ 01273 843235

Flint Acres Pig Farm. Every type of pork including dry cured bacon and gammon. Extremely reasonably priced, for example a hock bought for just £1 at Shoreham Market made a great pea and ham soup.

☎ 01798 831036 ☛ adcordery@tiscali.co.uk

Townings Farm rear pigs, Sussex angus beef and South Downs sheep. One of few suppliers of mutton and hogget, both of which make a wonderful stew. Also raise turkeys for Xmas. Find them at Lewes Market where they also sell chorizo from Beal's charcuterie.

☎ 01444 471352

Chanctonbury Game – Local game including wild rabbit, pheasant, pigeon, partridge, grouse, hare and every cut of venison. Supplies are dictated by the season. Find them at Shoreham Farmers' Market.

☎ 01903 877551

Standean Farm Butchers. Sourced directly from their farm near Ditchling. Ride out from Brighton and you can see their lambs in the fields. Daily deliveries to caterers.

☎ 01273 502838

Scalands Farm have been farming South Devon cattle for forty years, raising them on a natural grass-rich diet. The animals are slaughtered in the locality which reduces stress for the animals as well as the carbon footprint. The beef is dry-aged on the bone for at least 28 days, greatly improving the flavour.

☎ 01580 880414 ☞orders@scalandsfarm.co.uk

O'Hagan's sausages. Sausages used to be cheap and nasty food; you never wanted to enquire too deeply about what went into the filling. Now an amazing range of quality products are on offer. For Guy Fawkes this week, I got two dozen 'Brighton Bangers' from Clarks butchers on the Lewes Road. Not a drop of fat in the roasting tray when the bangers emerged from the oven.

O'Hagan's of Chichester take pride of place because of the alluring range of fillings. Sussex Savoury, Sweet Italian, Drunken Duck and Ostrich. The catalogue is also impressive for stating the exact percentage of meat in each sausage. Hot Mexican Pork rocks in at 95%.

☎ 01243 649133

Fresh Fish

Jem's Fresh Fish. Their boat fishes out of Newhaven, supplying a stall at the North Laine Farmers' Market in Diplocks Yard. Not much more than an alley way, Diplocks Yard used to supply barrows to the Steptoe & Sons of Brighton. Recently spruced up by the owners of Jessups Farm, it now hosts a Saturday market. The fish stall always has a terrific display of produce including scallops, squid and hot smoked salmon. Fishmonger Gavin is a stalwart Spurs supporter; the only fish shop with a crowing cockerel.

☎ 07541 031200 ☛ daly-j2@sky.com

<u>B&N Fish Sales.</u> An enviable display of fish at their shop next to the row of millionaire white houses on Portslade beach. The trawler docks right next door. Opulent range of fish and seafood, lobsters doing backstroke in a bubbling bath. Must confess to one wayward child feeding a copy of my Brighton book to the crustaceans. Open for retail sales as well as daily deliveries to caterers.

☎ 01273 430646 ☛ shop@bnfs.co.uk

<u>Sea Haze</u>. A little shop next to the Fishing Museum, manned by Neil and his trusty Polish lieutenant. On the beach is a seafood stall, with cockles, mussels, jellied eels and homecooked whelks. 'Sea Haze' is a tribute to Carol and Alan Hayes who opened the shop. Carol can trace her Brighton fishing heritage three hundred years, and Alan, the oldest fishermen in town, still gets up before the crack to shoot his nets and bring in the 'cetch.' Salt of the earth people.

☎ 01273 777007

Smoked fish & other smokers

Springs Smoked Salmon Their catalogue is far more extensive than simply smoked salmon, including reasonably priced cod's roe for taramasalata. Twice weekly deliveries to the trade.

☎ 01273 857338 ☛ sales@springssalmon.fsnet.co.uk

Lewes Smoke House. Lightly smoked trout, mackerel and honey roast salmon. Find them at Lewes Farmers' Market on a Friday.

☎ 0754 700 6067 ☛ info@thesmokehouselewes.co.uk

Weald Smokery A vast range of oak-smoked fish and meat, including smoked eel, kippers, lamb and venison. For special occasions, splash out on a hamper.

☎ 01580 879601 ☛ info@wealdsmokery.co.uk

V.J. Game. This supplier offers lots of smoked meat beyond local game. Bought some beautiful smoked ham at Shoreham farmers market, very reasonably priced.

☎ 01424 883060

Southdowns bacon & curers. John from Wilmington, a new arrival at Lewes Market. You would be hard pushed to find a better bacon.

☎ 01323 844160

Vegetables

These three farms produce muddy, misshapen vegetables that taste terrific.

Daylands Farm. Derek and Vicki's stall attracts an enormous queue at Shoreham Market. They also run 'Pick it, Cook it' events, where people forage the farm for edible produce, then concoct something tasty in the outside kitchen.

☎ 01403 711057 ☛ loucrush@pickitcookit.com

Noanah's Organics. An extensive choice of seasonal fruit and vegetables. Noanah is a welcoming presence at Lewes Market.

☎ 01273 890295

Laines Organic Farm. Salad produce that seems positively alive, and always something original like edible flowers or barley flour for baking.

☎ 01444 452480

Fruit farms, fruit juice and cider

Sussex used to be synonymous with apples before intensive agriculture led to the destruction of many orchards. Recent years have seen a revival of the tradition of cider making, using original strains of apple.

Tullens Fruit Farm – 6 varieties of apple juice. The orchard is grazed by the rare breed Dorset Down sheep, so lamb is also available from the farm shop.

☎ 01798 873800 ☛ sales@tullens.co.uk

Oakwood organic orchard. They used to produce fruit purely for eating, but following the blight of a terrible frost, they diversified into apple and pear juice.

☎ 01580 830893

Greenway Fruit farm has a good presence at farmers markets, selling apples, pears, plums and cherries.

☎01323 833118 ☛ grahamlove@tiscali.co.uk

Ringdens Farm apple juice made from 20 different varieties of apple.

☎ 01580 879385 ☛ sales@ringdenfarm.co.uk

Gran Steads ginger wine comes 'dark and mellow' or 'light and fiery.' They also make their own lemonade.

☎ 01273 452644 ☞ enquiries@gransteadsginger.co.uk

Appledram Farm – cider, perry and spicy ginger cordial. Produced on Pump Bottom Farm, an address that really belongs in Brighton.

☎ 01243 773828 ☞ info@appledram-cider.co.uk

Battle cider. Sweet, medium and dry, their cider livens up many a food festival. The dry is truly stunning.

☎ 01424 429588. ☞ andrew@battlecider.com

Wobblegate cider An inspired name, describing your walk after imbibing a drop too much.

☎ 01444 881356 ☞ info@wobblegate.co.uk

Non-perishable goods – jam, honey, chutney, mustard

Paynes Bee Farm. As well as a large range of honey, Paynes make jam, marmalade, pickle, chutney and a tasty honey dressing. Regular presence at farmers markets.

☎ 01273 843388 ☞ sales@paynes-beefarm.com

Brighton Pyrenees Honey. You may wonder where the Pyrenees feature on a map of the South Downs, but when available they source honey from Moulescoomb and Portslade.

☎ 07980 72187

Stratta fruit vinegars. John and Mary Stratton produce fruit vinegars with a light, refreshing taste. For many years John worked as catering manager at Brighton University, but has now carved out a thriving business with this original line in vinegar. You have a choice of more than twenty fruit to choose from.

☎ 07980 72187 ☞ stratta@btinternet.com

The Merchant Farmer, Jonathan Ffrench, produces a great selection of condiments, Sussex grainy mustard, rumpy cider marmalade and old fashioned fudge.

☎ 01892 783430 ☞ sales@themerchantfarmer.co.uk

Auntie Vals, the last word in preserves. Over 20 marmalades such as lemon & elderflower, chocolate orange and Bottle Wreck Porter. Jams made from old Sussex recipes like High Dumpsie Dearie made with plum, apple and pear.

☎ 01903 746748 ☞ sales@auntievals.com

<u>Bartie's Sussex Faire.</u> An imaginative line in chutney, relish & marmalade. Seville Devil marmalade; Spiced Beetroot Chutney; X-Tremely Serious Chilli.

☎ 01444 892376

<u>The Spice Company</u> – 'spices hand blended in Sussex.' Bought some of their enormous cardamon pods with black lustrous seeds like molten larva. Tasted mellow and smokey.

☎ 0845 3913374 ☛ paul@thespicecompany.co.uk

Local wine & beer

Sparkling wine from Sussex is the success story of the decade. We have a similar climate to the Champagne region, and French vintners are now vying for a slice of The Downs. We have chalk soil which enhances ripening by reflecting sunshine onto the grapes. Chalk also encourages drainage, protecting the roots from accumulation of rain. So barring wildly wet summers such as 2012, we have the perfect conditions for creating excellent sparkling wine. Indeed, Nyetimber and Ridgeview vineyards use the three classic champagne grapes – pinot noir, pinot meunier and chardonnay.

I never believed our climate was warm enough to produce an English red wine, until a visit to Hidden Spring Vineyard at Horam. They offered a taste of a terrific smoky number from Sandhurst vineyard. As you will see, reds have caught on. Most of these vineyards are in Sussex, with just the odd one across the border in Kent or Surrey. You can order direct from their websites.

Biddenden. White, red, rosé & sparkling wines, as well as cider and apple juice. The crisp fruity white is a firm favourite of the Mule.

☎ 01580 291726 ✓ www.biddendenvineyards.com

Bookers. White, red, rosé & sparkling. A café on the estate which also hosts harvest suppers.

☎ 01444 881575 ✓ www.bolneywineestate.co.uk

Breaky Bottom. Sparkling wine & kir royal. Peter Hall is a true pioneer having planted his vines in 1974. He won fame for white wines made from Seyval Blanc and Muller Thurgau grapes, but now concentrates on sparkling.

☎ 01273 476426 ✓ www.breakybottom.co.uk

Carr Taylor. White, rosé, sparkling & fruit wines including mead.

☎ 01424 752501 ✓ www.carr-taylor.co.uk

Davenport organic. Grapes are picked by hand at four different vineyards, each with distinctive terrain. White, red and sparkling wine.

☎ 01892 852380 ✓ www.davenportvineyards.co.uk

Lurgashall. Specialists in fruit wines including gooseberry, elderflower and rose petal. Also produce fruit liqueurs and seven types of mead.

☎ 01428 707292 ✓ www.lurgashall.co.uk

Nyetimber now has 400 acres of vines in West Sussex and Hampshire, devoted to producing first rate sparkling wine.

☎ 01798 813989 ✓ www.nyetimber.com

Old Tramway. Regular presence at Shoreham Market, with an affordable selection of wines. White, sparkling and also cider.

☎ 01737 551829

Ridgeview. The vineyard that accumulates prizes by the barrel load. They now produce ten varieties of sparkling wine. The tour is really instructive on how champagne is made, ending with an obligatory tasting.

☎ 01444 241441 ✓ www.ridgeview.co.uk

Sedlescombe Organic. The first organic English vineyard. A great selection – red, rosé, white, sparkling, fruit wine, fruit juice and cider.

☎ 0800 980 2884 ✓ www.englishorganicwine.co.uk

Sandhurst. White, rosé and red, they also brew beer with their own hops. There's a B&B on the farm – no problem finding a nightcap.

☎ 01580 850296 ✓ www.sandhurstvineyards.co.uk

Hammerpot brewery. Micro brewery near Arundel curiously located on a street called The Vinery. Tasted their Bottle Wreck Porter at a beer festival and it was really chocolatey.

☎ 01903 883338 ✓ www.hammerpot-brewery.co.uk

Harveys Brewery. Famous Sussex brewery; the tour is something of an institution. Most production goes towards Harveys Best, but there are also celebration ales for special occasions; Bonfire Beer, Christmas Ale and Tom Paine to celebrate Lewes's most famous son.

☎ 01273 480209 ✓ www.harveys.org.uk

W.J. King brewery. Horsham brewery established in 1860. A great selection of ales.

☎ 01403 272101 ✓ www.kingbeer.co.uk

Farm shops

As a simple townie I imagined that the pattern of country life was somewhat fixed in time. The example of Court Garden Farm Shop offers a cautionary tale. A few years ago I was commissioned to provide the dinner for an EU Festival of Biodiversity at Rye Town Hall. All ingredients had to be sustainable, and sourced from Sussex or Normandy. I collected my vegetables from Court Garden Farm Shop, at the end of Ditchling village. Prime asparagus, salads and herbs. Coming to write this piece I discovered the shop now closed. The farm still rears sheep, wisely bred from 'North of England Mules', but they have diversified into wine production and shut the shop. So in terms of local produce, we live in constantly evolving times.

The best farm shops showcase food they produce themselves, and the shop at Offham is a prime example. Took the lane from Pells Pool at Lewes, through a wood brightened by a tranquil stream, and Offham emerged quite immaculate with the obligatory Yew Tree cottage and pretty church. Lifted the latch on the church door to find a cellist rehearsing a Bach prelude, the bow soaring up and down with lightness and melancholy.

Parked the bike in the farm yard alongside three pens of pigs. One with a heap of newborn piglets, mama exhausted but attentive. The next was home to ten little porkers rolling in the straw. The final bunch were more your lazy adolescent, grunting at the back of the class. Inside the shop, a wonderful display of butchered meat, every cut of lamb, beef and (sadly) pork, coming from the farm. Sat outside in the warm November sun and and munched a beef and horseradish sandwich with a glass of organic pear juice. By the time I left, pen number two were taking a nap, ten lean little piggies all snuggled up close.

I first discovered Boathouse Organics as the bus sailed by to Uckfield. It has its own market garden and an abundance of seasonal produce. Meat is sourced from organic livestock across the county, and the animals are slaughtered at a small local abattoir. Such is their success, a second shop has recently opened in Lewes.

Farmers' Markets in Brighton lack longevity. There was a great one at Ralli Hall in Hove, but that slipped away. Others begin with a wealth of authentic produce, but gradually meat and vegetables give way to cupcakes and cookies. Perhaps the re-development of the London Road covered market holds potential for something fresh in the city.

There are two terrific markets within striking distance of Brighton. Shoreham is by unanimous consent the best in Sussex, with a wealth of fine produce comparable to the heart of Normandy. There is a real festive buzz about the place, a jazz combo with smouldering vocals, and a pub piano out on the street. Even when a winter storm blew the stalls away, the Community Centre opened its doors to the whole shebang, the hall packed and steaming. Make a note in your diaries for the second Saturday of every month.

Lewes Market is small but perfectly formed. Every Friday in the Market Tower, a real harvest festival takes place. Meat, game, cheese, fish, organic fruit and vegetables. Stunning bread from Glynde, chorizo from Upper Dicker and mackerel smoked 0.9 food miles away. An interesting feature is the number of stall holders who have arrived from foreign fields. Noanah and Toos of organic vegetable fame come from Zimbabwe and Holland. Biodynamic apple man is Spanish and chocolate man comes from my old stomping ground of Copenhagen. A cosmopolitan local market.

Here's a list of other food markets in Sussex:

Arundel: third Saturday of each month in the High Street.

Battle: third Saturday morning of every month, Battle Abbey Green.

Chichester: first and third Fridays of each month in East Street and North Street.

Eastbourne: last Saturday morning of the month in Ocklynge Road, Old Town.

Hailsham: second Saturday morning of every month at the Cattle Market.
Hastings: second & fourth Thursday of every month in Robertson Street.

Haywards Heath: second and fourth Thursday at The Orchards Shopping Centre.

Heathfield: third Saturday morning of the month in the Co-op car park.

Horsham: every Saturday in Carfax.

Lewes: first Saturday morning of every month in Cliffe Pedestrian Precinct.

Rye: every Wednesday morning at Strand Quay.

Steyning: first Saturday of each month in the High Street Car Park.

Uckfield: first Saturday morning of each month in Luxford Car Park.

Worthing: fourth Saturday of each month in South Street Square.

The Nosebag Awards

Recommending eateries is a notoriously difficult task. Chefs give way to exhaustion, restaurants fall foul of the Environmental Health and longevity is an ambition few can achieve. 'Coriander' for example, praised in the first chapter for its original grub is no more. So this Guide limits itself to just four recommendations.

The Coast Café, Worthing: About 400 yards east of the pier, where the prom gives way to the beach. Compared to the mayhem of Brighton in high season, this place offers absolute tranquility, where nothing disturbs the roll and hush of the sea. Good coffee, friendly service and simple food well done. An artist's studio adds colour to the place, and there's not the hint of a hill all the way back to Brighton. They've got a cunning marketing line: 'Sshh... Don't tell anyone.' Wouldn't dream of it.

☎ 01903 216937.

The Melrose Fish Restaurant, Brighton: Directly facing the West Pier, The Melrose offers old time hospitality. The simple faith of taking a booking without demanding your phone number. Recognition of old customers – a window seat, your favourite wine – because this is what we crave in life, to be plucked out of the grey crowd and made to feel we are special. The Mule being a creature of habit, always goes for scallops followed by grilled plaice. The crisp, chunky, sun-tanned chips are something to be savoured. An old fashioned dessert trolley stands centre stage, making no concession to standardized portion control, Level 3 piping skills or the epidemic of diabetes. Then there's that intimate view of the old pier, like the bare bones of a noble whale somehow defying the waves.

☎ 01273 326520.

The Ginger Dog, Brighton: Head for Kemptown and College Place is just south of the hospital gates. Imaginative menu that changes with the seasons. Fish, game, vegetarian – every dish is thoughtfully composed. Although it no longer resembles the original Wellington pub, you can still get decent beer at the bar. The service is professional without being starchy; quality grub without fiddle or fuss.

☎ 01273 620990

The Blue Man, Brighton began life as a tiny North African restaurant on Edward Street. Magreb menus in France have couscous and tagine but rarely anything else. Here were dishes of fish and game with vibrant combinations of flavour. The concept has now re-opened as a North African tapas bar just above the Clock Tower. The chef owner is Magi, an apt moniker as the new setting is a wonderful place with relaxed staff, warm colours and the fun of a cheeky fez. The music alone is worth the visit, with an Algerian version of 'Rock the Casbah' that outdoes The Clash.

☎ 01273 726003

Chapter 4

Les Produits du Terroir de Haute Normandie

In Sussex we are only just beginning to reclaim our connection with the land. In Normandy it is a tradition that has remained unbroken for centuries. This is partly because people still work on small farms in patchwork fields known as 'le bocage'. Partly because the concept of 'terroir' places local food and drink as central to their heritage. Visit any village on market day and the place will have peasants setting up shop with just a tray of eggs, a bucket of cream and bottles of brown apple juice that taste like the sun and the earth.

There are five important components to Norman cuisine – apples, pork, duck, fish and dairy produce. One of the joys of cycling around the 'bocage' is the <u>apple</u> <u>orchards</u> with their gnarled and wayward trees. Travel in April and the countryside is bright with apple blossom, finally tumbling to a carpet of pink and white petals. Much of the crop is made into cider, Calvados and a refreshing apéritif called 'pommeau.' Etienne Lurois has an organic orchard in the village of Saint Saire, just south of Neufchatel. Visit at harvest time, and the air is dense with the smell of fermenting apples, as wild yeasts get to work on the crushed fruit. There are tours of the farm, ending with a tasting in an ancient beamed barn. You can find out more on ☎ 02 32 97 10 74 ✓ www.closdubourg.pagesperso-orange.fr

Apples feature everywhere on the menu, alongside roast cod, pork or pheasant. Apple compote is a common accompaniment, cutting through the fat of a rich terrine. Calvados sorbet is the regional 'digestif', encouraging the old tummy to make room for the next course. Pride of place on the dessert trolley goes to the famous 'tarte normande.' There are as many recipes as there are restaurants, some with sweet pastry others puff; the best are topped with a layer of scorched apples that have seen serious action in the oven.

Dairy Country: Neufchatel is capital of Le Pays de Bray, the fields deeply green, cows clinging to the steep hillsides. The milk is turned into cream, butter, fromage blanc and a caramelised milk preserve known as 'confiture du lait.' Then there are the famous Normandy cheeses – Camembert, Pont l'Evêque and Neufchatel. Camembert is made from raw milk, and is particularly good when ripe. Pont l'Evêque comes from a little town south of Deauville in the Auge region which is also famous for calvados and beef. The cheese is surprisingly pungent for its mild flavour. Neufchatel has a life of its own, starting out creamy white and ripening to a yellow brown crust, like a parcel of old parchment containing cream of the gods. There's a little museum in the town devoted to the local cheese. Not far away at Bellencombre, the Bazin family produce a lovely 'fromage de chèvre', as snowy white baby goats romp in the straw. With all these Normandy cheeses, it's best to avoid the cold embrace of the fridge and let the beauties breathe.

<u>Pork</u>: Almost every village in Normandy has a charcuterie displaying the innermost parts of the pig. There are clusters of charcuteries in the main squares of Rouen, each one vying for the plumpest boudin noir and boudin blanc. In Dieppe, C.H. Normand a charcuterie close to the turning bridge, has a banner pronouncing 'Champion d'Europe de Boudin Blanc.' You can stock up there before catching the ferry, and encounter another famous Norman tradition, surly and disdainful service.

La Ferme de Peau de Leu is a pig farm at Somméry, and possibly the only one with its own charcuterie. Open on Fridays and Saturdays, Joel Bocquet sells quality meat at reasonable prices. He supplied 'Le Moulin de Mule' with leg of pork, boudin blanc and a tasty dried sausage. I used to have a kip on a banquette in the restaurant between lunch and dinner service, and once woke to find Joel waiting patiently, unwilling to disturb the slumbering chef.

☎ 02 35 09 81 00 ✓ www.viandefermenormandie.com

<u>Duck</u> appears on Norman menus as commonly as chicken. Majestic as 'magret', tender as 'confit', the illicit pleasure of foie gras. 'Canard à la Rouennais' is the signature dish of the region. It starts off grilled in the kitchen but then proceedings move to a gueridon trolley in the restaurant itself. The bird is dissected and the carcass crushed in a special press, the juices

combined in a sauteuse with calvados to form the sauce. This is performance art requiring great dexterity, and the waiter needs years of experience before acquiring the title 'maître canardier.' You can enjoy the whole experience at 'Les Quatre Saisons' opposite Rouen station. There may be an element of confusion when you ask for the bill.

With its long coastline and tidal rivers, the region teems with <u>fish and seafood</u>. The maritime history of Normandy is beautifully described at the Musée des Terre-Neuvas et de la Pêche at Fécamp, recounting perilous expeditions to Newfoundland in search of cod. See the catch being hauled in at Dieppe harbour, filleted by fishwives with tongues sharp enough to skin a huss. Enjoy the finished article at a dozen restaurants on Quai Henri IV, and for real crustacean lovers, sit down to a seafood platter at 'Aux Produits Fruit de Mer' on Pourville beach. The abundance of local scallops is a culinary treat, although an accompanying 'sauce normande' means they are simply smothered in cream.

Les Marchés Fermiers

I lived in the capital of Normandy for three years and can tell you it is not a happening place. One New Years Eve we stepped out of an African restaurant to discover absolute silence, not a greeting, not a firecracker, not a single pair of stilettos tripping down the street. Wind round to summer, and shutters are tightly closed hours before sundown, 'bonjour tristesse' and goodnight. Yet on market day people come to life, celebrating all that is good and true in their corner of Normandy. The Seine Maritime is just one half of Upper

Normandy, stretching from Le Havre in the West to Le Tréport in the East. It numbers one hundred and forty farmers' markets every week. Each village has its treasured market day, coming alive with the smell of straw and the sound of ragtime music. Here then is a market for every day of the week.

Buchy, lundi
Postcode 76750

Buchy is not much more than a scattering of houses around a crossroads about 20 kilometres east of Rouen. It is easily accessible by bike using the Amiens train from Rouen. The great thing about this market is that all the cattle come to town. Peasants too, and if you don't get into a restaurant early you won't find a seat. Nearby attractions are Forge-les-Eaux which has a museum to the Resistance in the Second World War, and a wonderful outdoor swimming pool. To the north is the pig farm and charcuterie described on the previous page. Not far south at Chapelle-St-Rouen, Dominique Camus brews Northmen Viking beer on his farm.
✓ www.northmaen.com

Duclair, mardi
Postcode 76480

The Seine meanders its way West of Rouen, in no hurry to meet the sea. The winding valley of the Seine is a delightful route to take, chalk cliffs rising with power and grace, thatched cottages sprouting plants along the roof. The region is famous for soft fruit and Monsieur Jourdaine who supplied my restaurant in Rouen, spoke of the strawberries in reverential tones. They had a sweetness and fragrance that needed no adornment. One loop in the river further along is the ruined Abbey of Jumièges, scene of Celtic music nights punctuated with cascading fireworks.

La Bouille, mercredi
Postcode 76530

Take the road from Rouen beneath the steep hillside of Canteleu. Clunking freight railway tracks and giant factory chimneys give way to scenes of tranquil boating trips, men in beards and boaters, ladies managing voluminous skirts. You can even pitch your picnic hamper in the shade of Flaubert's summer house. There is a lovely new cycle path from Croisset, landscaped with trees and rose bushes. A little red ferry carries you to La Bouille, a pretty village sheltering under a powerful cliff. You will eat well here among the artist galleries and artisan shops.

Arques-la-Bataille, jeudi
Postcode 76880

A bustling little village 10 kilometres south of Dieppe, easily reached on the 'Avenue Verte.' The views from the ruined castle on the hill are magnificent. Not far away at St. Nicolas d'Aliermont is the bee farm of Marc Fourneau. Open every day, the farm produces a wonderful range of honey and great slabs of honey cake.

☏ 02 35 85 83 86

Clères, vendredi
Postcode 76690

Clères sits on the little River Scie which weaves, ducks and disappears before emerging breathless at Pourville beach. Trains stop frequently on the Dieppe to Rouen line, and the market shelters under a vast open-sided barn. After filling your bags and paniers, enjoy lunch on the river bank at 'Le Clos de la Roseraie.' Then visit the 'parc zoologique' which is the most tranquil place on earth. Beautifully landscaped, the path traces the habitat of peacocks and pink flamingos before rising through ancient woodland with deer and kangaroos. The grounds of the castle play host to exhibitions of bold sculpture and fantasy art. Not a place to be missed.

✓ www.parcdecleres.net

Dieppe, samedi.

Dieppe Market is a festival of food and drink. All the countryside comes to town with a wonderful array of seasonal fruit and vegetables, lettuce bursting with life, honey, cheese, fish of course, hanging salami and cider. I love the phrase on the label of Longueville cider, 'naturellement troublé', a succinct reflection on modern life. Just one weekend in November the market is eclipsed by 'La Fête d'Harengs et Coquilles St Jacques.' Herrings are grilled in every street and restaurants prepare a scallop feast. The Festival poster is designed by Popey, an English artist resident in these parts, totally unrelated to Olive Oil. You can visit her workshop on the Rue de la Rade.

Rouen, dimanche

The panoramic view from my flat was one memory of Rouen I will never forget. The other was Sunday market at Place St Marc. My routine began with chestnut honey from Monsieur Fourneau, and logs of charcoal goat's cheese from Père Bazin. Then on to the salad stall for red and white radish, sharp scented tomatoes and fresh herbs sparkling with dew. Exchanged greetings with Monsieur Jourdaine who delivered vegetables in the week, and cast about for something a little different. Gleaming sea trout from the River Bresle, gooseberries for mackerel, Vitelotte potatoes with guinea fowl.

The café terraces around the square were absolutely packed, waiters twirling trays, clearing cups and counting out change like the winning hand at a dominoes match. Best of all was the aroma of cooking food. Spits turning with roasting chicken and duck, potatoes basting in the fat. Giant vats of seafood paella, ham risotto, plump sausages and sauerkraut. There was a vibrancy, a sense of theatre about the place, the commotion eventually subsiding as the mechanical cleaners snuffled up debris, and the antique traders wrapped their wares in jaundiced copies of *Paris Match*. Then Monday was like a real Sunday, and life in Rouen resumed its quiet pace.

Palmarès de bonne bouffe – Nosebag awards.

Something France has that we do not, are affordable restaurants for working men in need of midday sustenance – 'les restaurants routiers.' Solid, commanding women run the show, but the clientele is predominantly male, clad in blue overalls, generations of hard labour ingrained under the knuckles. We have working men's cafes with cooked breakfasts, but for real quality lunches at a reasonable price, you may have to visit France. Here are three good addresses.

La Chaloupe, Dieppe
Tucked away on Dieppe docks just a kilometre from the swing bridge. It offers incomparable value for money. Four courses and all you can drink for only 12 Euros. A more vivid description is provided in Chapter 1. 18 Cours de Dakar, 76200 Dieppe.
☎ 02 35 40 47 78.

Restaurant de la Mairie, Bois Guillaume
If you're heading from Rouen to Neufchatel, the road rises steeply, turns sharply past the former Maison de Mule, and finally levels out in the suburb of Bois Guillaume. After a large crossroads, the impressive town hall sits on the left, and opposite is this excellent restaurant. Ate a memorable wing of skate here. 3182 Route de Neufchatel, 76230 Bois Guillaume.
☎ 02 35 60 15 20.

Le P'tit Bistro, Petit Quévilly
Rouen's Rive Gauche is rarely visited by tourists as all the historic monuments are on the other bank, close to the Cathedral square. Most of this part of Rouen was destroyed by Allied bombing in 1944 and re-built in unspectacular

form. I enjoy cycling around the Rive Gauche as there is a completely different feel to the place, working class with a big North African presence. This little restaurant serves a good lunch and is close to the 'Jardin des Plantes.' Both are worth a visit. 97 Rue Louis Poterat, 76140 Rouen.

☎ 02 35 63 51 58

La Toque d'Or, Rouen

If you want to dine out in a bit more style, the Place du Vieux Marché has several old beamed restaurants flirting with Michelin stardom. The 'Toque d'Or' is less exclusive but

excellent value. I enjoyed scallops with girolles mushrooms on a three course menu costing just 18 Euros. 11 Place du Vieux Marché, 76000 Rouen.

☎ 02 35 71 46 29

Bon appétit!

Chapter 5

Recipes Based on Local Produce

Recipes based on local produce.

Many of these recipes have been contributed by local chefs and artisan producers. Together with offerings in the earlier book 'A Mule in Brighton – a Taste of The Downs', they form a kitchen repertoire rooted in Sussex. A big thank you to all who provided these excellent dishes.

- Martin Hadden, executive chef at Ockenden Manor in Cuckfield.
- Caroline & Louise from Daylands Farm in Steyning.
- Sam Linter chief vintner at Bolney Wine Estate.
- Tess Flower owner of the village shop at Upper Dicker.
- Sarah and Mark Hardy from the High Weald Dairy.
- Jeremy Smith from Scalands beef farm at Robertsbridge.
- Vicki Thorp of Hammerpot Brewery.
- Sam the Brighton lobster fisherman.
- Riad from the Wild Cherry Deli in Brighton.
- Elspeth Broady and Diane Harris from London Road station garden.
- Auntie Val of Pulborough chutney fame.
- Sarah Payne from Cocoa Loco.
- Moose from the Redroaster Coffee House.

Bon Appétit!

Soups and Starters

Pease Pottage – Thick Pea Soup

Pottage is the old name for the vegetable patch that produced a wholesome soup. Leeks, onions, peas, garlic were all grown in the pottage. Dried peas make for a cheap, nutritious and warming winter broth. This is a simple vegetarian recipe, but it can also be flavoured with a thick chunk of smoky bacon.

Ingredients: serves 8 portions
250 gm dried split peas
70 ml vegetable oil
2 large onions
6 garlic cloves
Salt & pepper
300 ml semi skimmed milk
Enough water to make a thick soup

Method
1 Peel the onions & garlic, chop and sweat down under cover in a little vegetable oil.

2 Add the peas, milk, a pint of water and seasoning. Bring to a simmer, and gradually stir in more water as the peas start to swell. Remember, you are aiming for a thick soup, so do not add too much water at once.

3 After an hour simmering, pass the soup in a blender, adjust for seasoning and serve.

Oriental Selsey Lobster nage

Martin Hadden, Executive Chef, Historic Sussex Hotels

This recipe reflects the best of modern English cooking. It centres on a supreme local product, Selsey lobster which colonises the rocky seabed off the West coast of Sussex. It then adds a taste of Thailand, because our kitchens are open to flavours from across the globe. And finally it recognises our debt to classical French cuisine with the word 'nage' which means broth.

Martin Hadden oversees the kitchens at three outstanding Sussex hotels. 'The Spreadeagle' at Midhurst, 'Ockenden Manor' in Cuckfield and 'Bailiffscourt' on the way to Climping beach. Ockenden Manor has a Michelin star, but the standard of cooking is so high at each hotel, it is difficult to know why all three kitchens have not received the Michelin accolade. www.hshotels.co.uk

Ingredients: serves 2

1x 2lb Selsey lobster cooked & sliced
250ml lobster and vegetable stock
1 tomato skinned and diced
2 spring onions finely shredded
Half a chopped chilli
Knob of fresh ginger finely shredded

Juice of 2 limes
2 Sticks lemon grass crushed
2 lime leaves
Soy sauce
Dash of Nam pla – Thai fish sauce
Tsp toasted sesame oil
Chopped fresh coriander

Method

1 Warm the lobster and vegetable stock. Add the ginger, chilli, soy sauce, sesame oil, nam pla, lemon grass and lime leaves. Infuse for 10 minutes.

2 Add the spring onion, tomato, lime juice and sliced lobster. Warm for one minute, add the coriander and serve the lobster with the fragrant broth.

***

Celeriac and apple soup.

Apples once assumed the same importance in Sussex as they do in Normandy. Most orchards were ploughed up by industrial agriculture, but there are signs of a renewal of this lost tradition. 'Brighton Permaculture' has renovated two orchards at Stanmer Park and revived old Sussex varieties such as 'The Duck's Bill', 'Tinsley Quince' and the 'Alfriston' cooking apple. Celeriac is a versatile vegetable commonly used in France, deserving greater popularity over here.

www.brightonpermaculture.org.uk

Ingredients: serves 8 portions
    1 celeriac
    2 sweet apples
    2 large onions
    70 ml vegetable oil
    300 ml dry cider
    A little salt & pepper

Method
1 Use a large knife to top & tail the celeriac, then carve away the thick skin. Chop the white celeriac into chunks.

2 Peel the onions and roughly chop. Quarter, core and roughly chop the apples, but do not peel.

3 Sweat down all these ingredients under cover in a little oil. Add the cider and a pint of water. Bring to a simmer, stirring occasionally. At first the celeriac feels chunky, but do not add too much water at once – the celeriac softens during cooking and you want to avoid a thin soup. Lightly season so as not to overwhelm the sweetness of the fruit.

4 After simmering for an hour, pass through a blender, adjust for seasoning and serve.

***

Nettle & wild garlic soup

In the early summer of 2012 I spent a magical few days at the Ferme Européene des Enfants at Grandcourt, in the Northern corner of Normandy. The farm includes wonderful old barns that are transformed into dormitories for groups of children during the school holidays. There is a wood for building cabins, a barn for mounting concerts, and all manner of natural resources for teaching sustainable living. The 18th century manor house is home to Véronique Barrois who created the whole show. Sheep and poultry colonise the grounds, principal among which are the geese who live long idyllic lives, masters of all they behold. A little commotion ensues at nightfall when they are ushered into Goose House, tucked under a duvet, safe from Mister Fox.

Each evening I cooked dinner for the workers on the farm, one night a vegetable strudel, the next a cheese soufflé. On the first day Madame Barrois did a tour of the grounds, collecting nettles and wild garlic for this soup. Nothing sharp or stinging in the taste but a lustrous green colour.

www.la-fee.org

76660 Grandcourt, 12 kilometres south of Le Tréport.

Ingredients: 6 servings

A big bunch of nettle heads

A bunch of wild garlic

2 large onions

3 large potatoes

80 gm Normandy butter.

Salt & pepper.

Method

1 Peel and chop the onions, garlic and potatoes. Sweat down under cover in the melted butter. Pour in about 2 pints of water, but be careful not to add too much liquid as the potatoes are the only ingredient providing body to the soup.

2 Season and bring to a gentle simmer. After twenty minutes add the nettles. Simmer for a further twenty minutes, blend and serve.

***

Cheese and Wild Garlic Scones
Daylands Farm, Steyning

Dayland Farm near Steyning has a reputation for producing quality fruit and vegetables at affordable prices. Carol and Louise run 'Pick It Cook It' days when wild plants growing around the farm are foraged and turned into something tasty. Ingredients may include hawthorn blossom, elderflower, rhubarb, rosehip, greengage and jostaberry – a cross between gooseberry and blackcurrant. A real hedgerow harvest. Carol recommends eating these wild garlic scones with a good bowl of soup.

www.pickitcookit.com

Ingredients – 8 scones
100g plain flour
100g rye flour
50g butter
200g cheese (cut into small dice)
2 tsp mustard powder
2 tsp baking powder
pinch of chilli flakes
handful of wild garlic leaves, finely chopped
1 large egg
4 tablespoons natural yogurt

Method

1 Set the oven to 200°c, gas Mark 6.

2 Mix together the dry ingredients and rub in the butter until it has almost disappeared. Stir through the cheese and wild garlic

3 Whisk together the egg and yogurt and mix into the rest of the ingredients to form a sticky dough. Transfer to a floured work top and knead lightly.

4 Roll out the dough to roughly 4cm thickness, divide into 8 and shape into rounds. Bake on a tray lined with greaseproof paper, for about 15 minutes. A tap on the bottom should produce a hollow sound when cooked. .

***

'Little Sussex' Sheep's Cheese with salad.
Bolney Wine Estate

Bolney Wine Estate was one of the first modern English vineyards, established in 1972. It has expanded from three to thirty nine acres and now produces red, white and sparkling wines in a state of the art winery. Chief vintner Sam Linter recommends their Lynchgate red for this cheese recipe. It also goes well with another local product, salt marsh lamb from the coastal grazing lands east of Rye. The Estate offers tours and tastings, and you can book up for a course on the making of sparkling wine. www.bolneywineestate.co.uk

You may want to try 'Sussex Gold' rapeseed oil for the salad dressing. It comes extra virgin or oak smoked, and has a similar nutritional profile to olive oil.

Ingredients: 4 portions
4 'Little Sussex' sheep's cheese from the High Weald Dairy

4 large fresh tomatoes

2 red onions

100 gm plain flour

2 eggs

200 gm breadcrumbs

150 ml rapeseed oil

1 lemon

Salt & pepper

Method:

1 Un-wrap the cheeses. Prepare three separate bowls with flour, beaten eggs and breadcrumbs. Lightly coat the cheeses with flour, dip in egg wash and finally roll in breadcrumbs.

2 Heat a frying pan with a little oil. Gently lower the cheeses into the pan and cook for approximately 2 minutes or until golden brown. Turn over and cook on the other side. Once complete place on kitchen paper to drain.

3 Slice the tomatoes, onions and finely chop the parsley. Place in a bowl and mix with lemon juice and seasoning. Drizzle with oil and mix well.

4 Serve the salad and fried cheese with some freshly toasted brown bread. Accompany with a glass of Bolney's Lychgate red wine.

***

Green Eggs & Ham
Upper Dicker Village Shop's Green Eggs & Ham

This bustling shop & café can be found in the village where 'Carry On' films were born. The breakfast menu boasts the 'Big Dicker', and the owner Tess Flower has an equally wonderful name, redolent of Thomas Hardy. Depending on the alignment of the moon, she slips into Madame Fleur mode, stiletto heels, black lace stockings and a red carnation clasped between her teeth.

The Village Shop, Coldharbour Road, Upper Dicker, BN27 3QE. Tel: 01323 844 352

'Based on the wonderful green herbs that grow on & around the Downs, we serve this popular dish in the café. The eggs are coloured & flavoured with a home made salsa verde.'

Ingredients per serving:
3 free range eggs
1 knob of butter
Slice of good, local ham
1½ tablespoons of Salsa Verde –see notes below
½ a bread roll
Salt & freshly ground pepper
Rocket leaves

Method:

1 Beat the eggs with some salsa verde, salt & pepper. Toast the bread roll and lightly butter.

2 Cook the green eggs in a pan with a teaspoon of butter, stirring constantly until cooked through.

3 Serve the eggs on top of the ham & toasted roll. Garnish the dish with a salad of rocket mixed with salsa verde & sea salt.

Sussex Salsa Verde

Take a handful of parsley & a selection of fresh herbs, grown or foraged. Dill, oregano, rosemary, or savory which is a leaf similar to sage. Wild marjoram grows plentifully around here, or you could also use wild garlic which I always pick when visiting The Long Man of Wilmington.

Whizz together with enough olive oil to make a pesto-like consistency. Add salt & pepper to taste. This will last well in the fridge for 2 or 3 weeks.

***

Sussex Smokies with Tremains Cheddar
The High Weald Dairy

The High Weald Dairy has been winning prizes for organic cheese for more than twenty years. Renowned for their variety of sheep cheeses, they also make cheese from cow's milk, including the cheddar in this recipe. The latest addition to their range is a 'Brighton Blue.' The dairy is near West Hoathly where chef Max Leonard created this recipe at the village pub.

Tel: 01825 791630

www.highwealddairy.co.uk

Ingredients: 4 ramekins for a starter

150 gm grated Sussex cheddar

250g Smoked Haddock from 'The Weald Smokery'

1 leek diced and sweated.

2 tablespoons chopped parsley & chives

150ml double cream

150ml whole milk

20 gm butter

20 gm plain flour

Handful of breadcrumbs.

Method:

Set the oven to 180°c, gas mark 4.

1 Poach the smoked haddock in milk and cream on a gentle heat for 3–5 minutes. Remove the fish and break into large chunks.

2 Melt 20 gm butter in a saucepan and stir in 20 gm flour to make a 'roux.' Gradually stir in the liquid used to poach the haddock until thickened.

3 Add 100 gm grated Sussex cheddar and mix well. Stir in the leek, herbs and haddock.

4 Mix 50g cheddar with the breadcrumbs. Fill each ramekin with the haddock mixture and top with cheesy breadcrumbs. Bake for 10–15 minutes.

5 Serve with warm crusty bread or croutons. You could also place a poached quail's egg on top.

***

Mackerel Mousse

The Sussex kitchen has its roots in the sea. Old prints of Brighton show fishing boats being hauled up the beach, the catch lifted by pulleys through manholes in the Arches, to be sold fresh on the Prom. Fishwives carried the catch inland in wide-brimmed baskets known as 'juggs.' Dog-drawn carts delivered the fish further afield, to Alfriston, Hassocks and Cuckfield. Every year towards the end of April, large shoals of mackerel arrived off Brighton Beach. Mackerel nets were blessed by a priest in a custom known as 'bending in', the boat owners providing cheese and beer for the fishermen and their families. The blessing of the nets has been revived during the Brighton Festival in May.

Mackerel is just about the most nutritious food, bursting with Omega-3 oils. By way of compensation, nature makes them dense with ticklish bones, so take care when doing the filleting.

Ingredients: 6–8 servings.
3 good sized mackerel

3 spring onions

Juice of 1 lemon

70 ml dry white wine

1 large tablespoon of Downsview double cream or Plaw Hatch yoghurt.

Salt & pepper

Method:

1 Set the oven to 180°c, gas mark 4. Clean the fish and lay in a lightly oiled oven tray. Cover with foil and bake for 30 minutes.

2 Carefully remove the skin and bones and place the flesh in a food processor with the finely diced onion and all the other ingredients. Blend for 20 seconds, scrape down and then blend again for another 20 seconds.

3 Serve with warm toast or brioche. Optional wasabi or horseradish cream.

***

Scallops in hock jelly

The Normans introduced 'jelly' to Sussex with a dish of poached pig set in its own gelatine. The hock used in this recipe is really rich in gelatine. Normally I never mess around with scallops, just a swift sear in the frying pan and they're done. However, I once got hold of some scallops five days before a dinner party, and thought that setting in jellied stock would be a good means of preservation. Hence scallops in hock stock was born.

Scallops were once food of the poor, boats sailing up the River Ouse to sell the catch from Cliffe Bridge in Lewes. Chinkerberries were a variety caught from a stretch of seabed off Chanctonbury Ring. I have never knowingly come across them, but a small local scallop called queenies can still be found.

Ingredients: serves 6
12 good sized scallops
1 hock of ham, smoked if available
200 ml dry white
Galingale, cloves, black peppercorns.
1 lemon
1 large onion

Method:

1 Place the hock in a big pan, cover with water and add a few peppercorns, cloves and a chopped onion. The Normans flavoured their jelly with galingale, a lemony root similar to ginger. You can buy it at 'Yum Yum' in Brighton's North Laine.

2 Bring the pan to a simmer and skim off the scum. When about a quarter of the water has evaporated add the wine. Simmer for 2 hours, occasionally turning the hock. Remove the hock, and strain the stock into a bowl.

3 Set the oven to 170°c, gas mark 4. Remove the red coral from the scallops, and cut the white part in two. Place white meat and the coral into an ovenproof dish, sprinkle with seasoning and lemon juice. Pour over enough hock stock to just cover the seafood. Cover with foil and cook in the oven for 15 minutes. Turn into a bowl, allow to cool and put in the fridge to set.

4 Bone the hock and cut the meat into small pieces, discarding any tough bits. Place the meat in a bowl, cover with hock stock and leave to set in the fridge overnight.

5 For service, take the hock and scallop jellies, and place one big spoonful of each onto 6 plates. Accompany with a crisp endive and lamb's lettuce salad.

***

Meat Dishes

Leg of Southdowns Lamb
Cooked in hay

You could source this recipe direct from Offham Farm shop which sells lamb from their own Southdown flock. They might also help you out with a bundle of hay, or ask one of the happy porkers in the yard to roll over and spare you a handful.

I learnt this method of cooking from the great French chef Michel Guérard. Strange as it may seem, the hay can overwhelm the flavour of the meat, so in this recipe the lamb is covered in hay for just 30 minutes. As there are no juices left in the roasting tray to make a gravy, a moist potato dish is suggested along with an aubergine and tomato compote.

Ingredients: 6–8 people

1 leg of lamb
Seasoning
Hay!

For the braised potato:
600 gm old potatoes
1 onion
1 leek
1 branch of rosemary
Lamb stock

For the stewed aubergine:
2 aubergines
1 onion
1 tin chopped peeled tomatoes
80 ml olive oil

Method:

Set the oven to 210°c, gas mark 7.

1 Season the lamb, place in a roasting tray and put in the hot oven for 15 minutes. Turn down the heat to 190°c, gas mark 5, and cook for a further 30 minutes.

2 Remove the lamb from the roasting tray, toss in some handfuls of hay, replace the lamb and cover with more hay. You could also add rosemary or garlic to the mix. Sprinkle about 200 ml water over the hay and return the roasting tray to the oven. The meat should be cooked after a further 30 minutes; a small knife inserted in the centre of the joint will reveal if further cooking is required. If you have a temperature probe, aim for 65°c. Remove the meat and leave to rest for half an hour.

3 The potato dish can be placed in the oven along with the lamb. Peel and thinly slice the potatoes. Place in a casserole along with the chopped leek and onion. Sprinkle with seasoning and half fill with hot lamb stock. Cover the casserole and place in the oven for 45 minutes. Stir the potato mixture and return to the oven uncovered for about another 45 minutes.

4 For the stewed aubergine, peel the onion and sweat down in some olive oil. Cut the aubergines in half lengthways, and divide each half lengthways again. Slice thinly and add to the saucepan with some seasoning. Cook under cover, stirring occasionally. When the ingredients have softened to a pulp, add the tomatoes and cook gently for 30 minutes.

5 Carve the lamb and serve with the potato and aubergine accompaniments.

***

Sussex Stewed Steak
Scalands Farm, Robertsbridge

The beef from Scalands Farm is dry-aged for at least four weeks producing an exceptional flavour. They use it to make Steer & Beer Pie for local pubs and restaurants, with stout from the Old Dairy Brewery. They recently widened their portfolio of products, smoking bacon, salmon and cheese, as well as offering specialist charcuterie and sausages. Jeremy who runs the farm, heroically broke away from calving to dispatch this recipe.

www.scalandsfarm.co.uk

'This is an old recipe which seems to have been passed around friends and family over generations. Whilst there are many different versions we have had particular success with this one. All measures are fairly approximate and this is a real "just chuck it all in" dish. The most important thing is to check the texture of the sauce and serve the beef when it reaches a nice thick consistency. If you feel the need to reduce the sauce on the hob towards the end of cooking, make sure you remove the beef and let it rest while you do so.'

Ingredients: serves 4 to 6

2 kilos of chuck steak in a single piece, or use any stewing steak such as blade or flank with some of its own fat.

2 medium onions

3 tablespoons of flour

250 ml port

250 ml strong dark ale such as Harveys Old Sussex

4 tablespoons of mushroom ketchup ('George Watkins' label)

Healthy pinch of salt and a few good twists of black pepper

Method:

1 Season the piece of meat and coat generously with flour. Place in a shallow baking dish that just fits the meat, and cover with slices of onion. Mix together the port, ale and mushroom ketchup, pour over the meat and seal with foil.

2 Place in a low oven for three to four hours.

***

Oxtail Casserole

Sussex cattle are derived from oxen that once worked the High Weald; a heritage that can be enjoyed with a hearty dish of oxtail. Recent years have seen growing popularity for cheaper unfashionable cuts of meat, cooked long and slow. The end product is tender and succulent, and like so much in cookery, the explanation lies in food science. Those parts of an animal with well developed muscles have lots of connective tissue which contains collagen. When collagen is cooked at a high heat in dry conditions, the protein coagulates creating toughness. If however, the meat is cooked gently in the presence of moisture, the collagen melts away as gelatine and the prospect of tough chewy meat disappears.

Ingredients: serves 4 people

1 kilo of oxtail

300 ml red wine

300 ml water

2 of the following – carrots, parsnips, onions, garlic cloves.

Salt and pepper.

Method:

1 Set the oven to 150°c, gas mark 2.

2 Peel and chop the vegetables. Put in a large casserole with the oxtail, wine and water. Season, cover with a lid and cook in a low oven for four hours.

3 Serve with mashed potatoes.

***

Starshot Ham with Mustard Cream Sauce
Hammerpot Brewery

Hammerpot is a micro-brewery near Chichester producing beers with names reflecting the local heritage. 'Red Hunter', an early aircraft that broke speed records flying over Littlehampton beach. 'Madgwick Gold', a corner of Goodwood racetrack, and 'Bottle Wreck Porter' evoking ships lost at sea. This beer won the CAMRA award as best porter in the south east, and is an ingredient for the mustard cream sauce. The ham is cooked in their 'Shooting Star' ale.

www.hammerpot-brewery.co.uk

Ingredients:

1 joint of ham
1 bottle Hammerpot 'Shooting Star Ale'
6 shallots
4 cloves, paprika, salt & pepper

For the sauce:
50 ml olive oil
2 shallots
300 ml double cream
'Bottle Wreck' porter mustard
200 ml cooking jus
Fresh parsley, salt & pepper

Method:

The ham can be cooked in a slow cooker or a low oven.

1 Chop six shallots and lay in the bottom of an oven-proof dish. Score the fat of the ham and rub all over with paprika, salt & pepper. Stud with cloves and place on top of the shallots. Pour over the Shooting Star Ale and a little water, depending on the size of the ham. Cook gently for six hours, or until the ham falls apart with a prod.

2 Dice a couple of shallots and sweat off in a pan with a drizzle of olive oil until soft. Add a splash of the ham cooking liquid, two good sized teaspoons of mustard and some seasoning. Bring to the boil, add the cream and simmer till thickened. Add the chopped parsley and serve with the ham.

***

Fish Dishes

Dover Sole
René Lebon, 'Aux Produits de la Mer.'

Pourville is an unspoiled beach nestling between the cliffs of Varengeville and Dieppe. A tractor hauls the fishing boats up the steep bank of pebbles, and the catch is unloaded for sale at a fish stall alive with local gossip. The kitchen of 'Aux Produits de la Mer' specialises in seafood. It has remained in the same hands, LeBon father and son, since 1948. There are a few rooms above the restaurant, with a twilight view of the tide retreating across an expanse of sand. The profile of the cliffs at sunset was captured by many of the great Impressionists. Four kilometres further West is the ancient castle of Jehan Ango and the beautiful Parc des Moutiers .

Rue du 19 Août, 76550 Pourville sur Mer, 5 kilometres west of Dieppe. Tel: 0033235843834 rene.lebon0824@orange.fr

Ingredients: serves 4

4 medium sized Dover sole – choose your sole at 'Les Barrières', the legendary fish market at the port of Dieppe.

20 gm butter

20 ml olive oil

50 gm flour

2 cloves of garlic

2 sticks of rhubarb

3 leeks

1 red pepper, seeds removed

500 gm potatoes

Turmeric, salt & pepper

Method:

1 Set the oven to hot.

2 Peel the potatoes, sprinkle with turmeric and steam.

3 Remove the skin from the sole and lightly flour on both sides. Add a knob of good butter and a drizzle of olive oil to a frying pan and heat until the butter turns light brown. Cook the fish for 2–3 minutes on each side over a gentle heat.

4 Cut down the length of the backbone, and place the pan in a hot oven with the door ajar. The fish are cooked when no blood can be seen on the bone.

5 Finely chop the leeks, rhubarb and red pepper. Steam for two minutes, then toss in a frying pan with a little olive oil, garlic, salt & pepper.

6 Serve the fish on the bed of vegetables with potatoes and a little lemon butter.

***

Squid tagliatelle
with tomato and coriander sauce

When I opened for business on Brighton beach, I naively thought the only local fish would be plaice, mackerel or cod. In fact there were loads of bream in the summer that tasted terrific scorched on the chargrill. Turbot, brill, guernard, pollock and one hot summer parrot fish! Most surprising was the availability of squid, something I had associated with southern Europe. Cuttlefish, a similar species, also made an occasional appearance. The sheath enclosing the innards was once used for quill pens; the black ink used to ward off predators completed the writing kit. The trick with both squid and cuttlefish is to cook them gently in an abundant sauce; this avoids the rubbery rings that bounce out of too many kitchens.

Ingredients: 6 portions

1 kilo cuttlefish	200 gm mushrooms
2 large onions	1 bunch coriander
4 cloves garlic	200 ml dry white wine
100 ml olive oil	50 ml double cream
1 tin peeled chopped tomatoes	Salt, pepper & tabasco
	500 gm dried tagliatelle
1 lemon	

Method:

1 Cut the head off the squid, retaining the tentacles. Cut along the tubular body and remove the innards in one fell swoop. Rinse the fish under a cold tap, then slice thinly along with the tentacles.

2 Finely chop the onions and garlic and sweat down in olive oil. When softened, add the squid and cook gently under cover. After 5 minutes add the wine, lemon juice, tomatoes, coriander and seasoning. Continue cooking on a low heat for 30–40 minutes. Meanwhile, slice the mushrooms and add for the last 10 minutes cooking. Finish the sauce with a dash of cream.

3 Cook the pasta, drain and serve with the calamari sauce. Garnish with a twist of lemon and sprig of coriander.

***

Scallop Pudding
Sam, Brighton lobster fisherman

Sam is one of a small tenacious band of fisherman who work their boats from Brighton Marina. A few years ago I joined him on a trip, harvesting the catch from lobster pots along the coast. I got a tiny insight into the hard and dangerous work of a professional fisherman. Sam is a great cook, using abundant produce from his allotment. This dish, like many traditional Sussex recipes, is cooked in a pudding basin.

'As a young man I worked on trawlers working the length of the Channel and North Sea. Scallops were a 'stocker' (crew perks), as were prawns and crabs which also found their way into the pot. This pudding was dished up two or three times a week. We were also dished up skate cheeks boiled in sea water with North Sea sauce – mustard powder mixed with vinegar. Lovely!'

Ingredients: 4 portions
    24 scallops
    250 gm smoked streaky bacon
    200 gm fresh breadcrumbs
    Milk – enough to moisten the pudding
    100 gm butter
    100 gm cheese

Method:

1 Set the oven to 190°c, gas mark 5.

2 Grease a large pudding basin with butter, and line with a layer of breadcrumbs. Cut the scallops into discs, and place some in the pudding basin along with the roes. Add some bacon and cover with breadcrumbs.

3 Fill the pudding basin with alternate layers of ingredients. Pour some milk over the last layer, just enough to be absorbed but not to cover the ingredients. Then finish with a coat of breadcrumbs dotted with butter and grated cheese. Put in the oven for 20 minutes or until browned.

***

Cod Mornay

This is a simple fish dish which I learnt as a commis chef at Michel's Brasserie in Oxford. Michel was an extravagant figure, a flirtatious Maître D, an unpredictable boss who introduced me to a repertoire of good brasserie food. Returning late one night without his key, he attempted a fateful entry into his upstairs flat via the glass roof of the restaurant extension. We last met at a seminar for 'sous-vide cuisine', a technological approach to cooking made famous by the Roux brothers. Michel's astonishment at my elevation from humble commis to chef lecturer was broadcast across the suited gathering in uncompromising Anglo-Saxon.

Prime ingredients for this dish can be found on either side of the Channel. In Sussex you could use Bookhams butter and any hard local cheese. If returning from France, stock up on Normandy butter, and a well aged Camembert or Neufchatel cheese.

Ingredients: serves 4

  600 gm cod fillet
  Juice of half a lemon
  70 ml dry white wine
  30 gm butter
  30 gm plain flour
  500 ml semi-skimmed milk
  150 gm cheese
  A good teaspoon of Dijon mustard
  Salt & pepper

For the Duchesse potato:
600 gm King Edwards or Maris Piper spuds
30 gm butter
50 ml semi skimmed milk

Method:

1 Set the oven to 190°c, gas mark 5.

2 Boil and mash the potatoes with a little butter, milk and seasoning. Set aside.

3 Divide the cod fillet into 4 portions and lay in an ovenproof dish. Season and moisten with wine & lemon juice.

4 Melt the butter in a pan and add the flour to make a roux. Cook gently for 2 minutes, and gradually stir in the milk. Add the mustard while still quite thick.

5 Simmer gently for 10 minutes. If using a hard cheese, grate and stir in off the heat, then coat the cod with sauce. If using a creamy Normandy cheese, roughly chop and scatter over the fish, then coat with the bechamel sauce. Bake for 20 minutes.

6 Pipe the Duchesse potatoes either directly onto plates, or into whirls on a baking sheet. Warm in the oven and serve with the cod mornay and a crisp salad.

***

Vegetarian Dishes

Spinach and samphire roulade with red pepper sauce.

Foraging has come of age with the renaissance in local produce, with 'wild' edible plants appearing in shops and restaurants. Samphire, once abundant on the cliffs that border the Seven Sisters, is now available in fishmongers during the summer. It has the haphazard shape of little green TV aerials, is slightly crunchy and salty as the sea. Other plants may once again find their place in the Sussex kitchen. The roots of sherdoone, a thistle found in hedgerows, were cut into lengths and boiled like asparagus. Hops and dandelion leaves were used in salads, dandelion plants sometimes hidden from the sun to produce a white leaf. This recipe provides a nice combination of colours, the green and white roulade set on a red pepper sauce.

Ingredients: 6 portions
Roulade:
600 gm fresh spinach
2 egg yolks
4 egg whites
Salt & pepper
Ground nutmeg
30 gm butter

Filling:

500 gm low fat fromage blanc

200 gm samphire

Sauce:

2 large red peppers

1 tin chopped, peeled tomatoes

2 onions

Method:

1 To make the red pepper sauce, chop the onions and de-seeded peppers and sweat down in a little oil. Stir in the tomatoes, season and simmer gently under cover for 30 minutes. Blend in a food processor, turn into a bowl and leave to cool.

2 Heat the oven to 190°c, gas mark 5. Lightly grease a baking tray and line with lightly buttered greaseproof paper. Cut out 2 more lengths of greaseproof and set aside till later.

3 Remove any thick spinach stalks, wash the spinach and briefly sweat down in a saucepan. Once softened, tip into a colander and leave to cool. Squeeze out any excess liquid and finely chop the spinach.

4 Put the spinach in a bowl and beat in the egg yolks, nutmeg and seasoning. In a separate bowl, whisk the egg whites to soft peaks. Turn the spinach mixture on top of the egg whites, and carefully combine with a large spoon. Pour out into the baking tray and spread thinly.

5 Bake for approximately 5 to 7 minutes – the sponge should be set but still springy. Place the baking tray on a cooling wire. After a couple of minutes, cover with a sheet of greaseproof paper and turn upside down onto the cooling wire. Carefully peel off the first sheet of greaseproof paper. When still slightly warm, cover with a new sheet of greaseproof and roll up into a swiss roll. Leave to cool.

6 Unroll the sponge, remove the greaseproof and spread with fromage blanc. Sprinkle with samphire and roll up again; leave to set in the fridge.

7 The roulade is refreshing served cold in high summer, otherwise warm in the oven. Serve sliced on a plate coated with red pepper sauce.

***

Beetroot Polenta
'Wild Cherry' Natural & Organic Deli

'Wild Cherry' is the jewel in the crown of Brighton food shops, sitting on top of Queens Park Road. It is a gastronomic cornucopia, every inch of the little shop packed with golden jars of honey, exotic cooking oils, artichoke stalks that are somehow succulent. Many of the vegetables are sourced from local allotments, including the beetroot in this recipe. The kitchen produces a wealth of original dishes inspired by Palestinian cuisine and there is also a strong line in healthy eating. This polenta recipe is rich in iron and vitamin C and also gluten-free. The café offers a sumptuous Middle Eastern breakfast and a novel range of homemade cakes. Mr & Mrs Hawa who run the shop, have been 'Brighton & Hove Foodie Award' finalists for the past three years. You can discover more on
www.wildcherrybrighton.co.uk

Ingredients: serves 4

250 gm coarse polenta

1 large onion

2 large raw beetroots cubed into 1 cm size

1 tsp ground cumin

Half teaspoon of salt & pepper

2 tablespoons olive oil

1 litre cold water

1 handful of Omega 4 seed mix for the topping

Method:

1 Pre-heat the oven to 180°c

2 Place all the ingredients in a large mixing bowl and combine well. Turn into a deep ovenproof dish. Scatter the seed mix on top.

3 Place in the oven for 40 minutes. Check if set – you want the polenta to remain a little moist. Remove from the oven, leave to stand for 5 minutes and serve.

Accompany with tomato sauce or salsa and a mixed leaf salad. Enjoy!

****

Tomato tartlets with frisée lettuce & walnut salad
London Road Station Garden

London Road station has long been important to The Mule as departure point for the Dieppe ferry. Slide the bike onto the train, cycle off at Newhaven past the Keystone Kop at border control and into the hold of the ship. Otherwise, it has been a place of little note, Nick the station master quietly running things these past twenty five years. Then something quite magical happened. The derelict scraps of land that bookend the ticket office were transformed into fertile gardens. A mini orchard of apples, plums and pears, bright yellow courgettes defying the lack of sun, and a public herb patch where commuters can brighten their evening meal with rosemary and thyme. A little eco triumph.

'At the end of September we always have frisée lettuces growing well in the garden. They seem to thrive on our chalky soil. The tomato tartlets are a delicious way of using up our final tomato harvest. We also grow basil and marjoram which work so well with the sweet flavour of the cherry tomatoes. The tartlets and frisée salad make a lovely summer lunch.'

http://londonrdstationpartnership.wordpress.com

Ingredients – approximately 12 tartlets

Pastry:

250 gm plain flour

Pinch of salt

100 gm cubed butter or half lard

2–3 tablespoons cold water

Filling:

30 sweet cherry tomatoes

1 sliced onion

Crushed garlic

Chopped basil or marjoram

Salad:

1 large frisée lettuce

200 gm chopped walnuts

Dressing:

1 tsp Dijon mustard

1 tsp honey

3 tablespoons walnut oil

1 tablespoon balsamic vinegar

1 crushed garlic clove

Method:

1 Preheat the oven to 180C gas mark 4.

2 Place flour, butter and salt in a large mixing bowl. With your fingertips, rub the butter into the flour until the mixture looks like breadcrumbs. Add the water, and use a cold knife to bind the dough. Wrap in cling film and chill for 30 minutes.

3 Butter a tartlet baking tray. Unwrap the pastry and roll out to 0.5cm thickness. Cut out small discs and press into the tartlet moulds. Bake for around 15 minutes or until starting to go golden brown.

4 For the filling, remove the tomato skins and chop. Melt the butter gently (or use olive oil) and add the onion and garlic. Cook for a few minutes to soften and then add the tomatoes & herbs. Slowly allow the mixture to reduce to a kind of 'jam.' Taste the mixture and adjust seasoning – if a little acid add some sugar.

5 Spoon the mixture into the tartlet cases. You can top with parmesan or crumbled goat's cheese if desired. Heat in the oven for about 5 minutes.

6 Rub the salad bowl with a crushed garlic clove and add the rest of the garlic to the vinaigrette ingredients. You can also add bacon strips to the salad – the classic French 'frisée aux lardons'- or crumble in some strong blue cheese. Dress the lettuce and walnuts with vinaigrette and serve with the warm tartlets.

***

Carrot & mushroom gateau with asparagus sauce

The asparagus season provides a luxurious introduction to summer. Those tender spears breaking through the earth's crust provide a wealth of aphrodisiac imagery. South Brockwells Farm near Uckfield has been growing asparagus for fifteen years, and supplies farmers markets at Shoreham, Steyning and Haywards Heath. In the winter their attention turns to providing all manner of game from the farm shop.

Ingredients: 4 portions
   600 gm carrots
   2–3 eggs (enough to bind the other ingredients)
   25 gm butter
   50 gm grated gruyère
   1 teaspoon honey
   fresh chervil
   2 shallots
   150 gm mushrooms
   40 ml sunflower oil

   Asparagus sauce:
   1 bunch asparagus
   1 small tin asparagus
   100 ml double cream
   Seasoning & ground nutmeg

Method:

1 Preheat the oven to 190°c, gas mark 5. Grease a soufflé dish and line the base with greaseproof paper.

2 Remove the woody stalks from the asparagus. Tie the bundle with string and stand the bottom half of the asparagus in a pan of boiling water. Simmer for 10 minutes, remove the string and simmer the whole bunch for a further 10 minutes. Drain the asparagus and remove the tender spears. Place the bottom half of the asparagus into a food processor with the cream, nutmeg and canned vegetables. Blend, season to taste and pour into a saucepan.

3 Peel and chop the carrots. Place in a small pan, barely half cover with water and add a knob of butter, seasoning and teaspoon of honey. Cook until almost all the liquid has evaporated and turn into a bowl. When cool enough to handle, roughly chop the carrots and set aside.

4 Whisk the eggs in a bowl with the carrot liquid, chopped chervil and grated cheese.

5 Finely chop the shallots and mushrooms and sweat down in a little oil. Combine well with the carrots and egg mixture, pour into the soufflé dish and cover with aluminium foil. Cook in the oven for 20 minutes in a bain marie of hot water. Remove the foil and cook for a further 20–30 minutes, until the gateau is almost firm. Turn out the gateau, serve with asparagus sauce and decorate with the tender spears.

***

Auntie Val's
Cheese & Chutney Tart

Auntie Val produces a great range of jams, marmalades and chutneys in her kitchen near Pulborough. All ingredients are locally sourced, the marrows for this chutney come from Jim's garden in Cootham. Marrow was once a traditional Sussex ingredient, combined in a pie with sugar, ginger, currants and sultanas. www.auntievals.com

Ingredients: 8 slices
    500 gm tomatoes
    200 gm puff pastry
    100 gm Plaw Hatch vintage cheddar
    1 jar Auntie Val's Marrow & Red Tomato chutney
    1 egg
    A good handful of cooked peas or beans.

Method:
1 Heat the oven to 200°c, gas mark 7, and grease a baking tray.

2 Roll out the puff pastry into a rectangle, overlapping the tray by a good inch. Lift the pastry onto the tray. Cover with sliced tomatoes and any cooked vegetables you might have in the fridge – this is a great recipe for using up leftovers. Spoon over a generous quantity of Auntie Val's Marrow & Red Tomato Chutney. Sprinkle with grated cheese.

3 Fold the overlapping pastry over each side and brush with egg wash.

4 Bake in the oven for 25 minutes. Serve hot or cold.

***

Desserts

Strawberry & Chocolate Cream Éclair

Every Normandy pâtisserie displays lustrous rows of chocolate scented with orange and ginger, filled with apple and calvados, crowned with the insignia of Guillaume le Conquérant. Each morsel transported with silken gloves and tweezers, then weighed on carefully calibrated scales as if containing carats of gold. The wrapping that follows is an art form requiring a college diploma and total disregard for the tourist waiting in the queue. We are not yet a match for the Normans, but Cocoa Loco and Montezumas are evidence of new-found chocolate success.

Choux pastry is a thing of wonder, that begins with fat melting in water and somehow ends in a light pastry shell. Complete the treat with thick cream from Downsview or Northiam Dairy, and fresh fragrant strawberries.

Ingredients: 8 éclairs
250 ml water
100 gm Bookhams unsalted butter
130 gm strong flour (50% Doves Farm light wholemeal works fine)
3 eggs

1 punnet strawberries

1 pint double cream

200 gm dark couverture – Montezuma and Cocoa Loco sell chocolate couverture with 73% cocoa solids.

Method:

1 Set the oven to 200ºc, gas mark 6. Pour the water into a pan and bring to the boil.

2 Roughly chop the butter and melt in the boiling water. Turn down the heat and stir in the flour. Beat vigorously for 30–60 seconds, then turn into a mixing bowl. When tepid, thoroughly beat in the eggs one at a time. Scrape the mixture into a piping bag and pipe fat cigar shapes onto a baking tray.

3 Bake for approximately 30 minutes. If a minute after removing from the oven the éclairs feel a bit soft, return to the oven till crisp. Place on a cooling wire.

4 Melt the couverture over a bowl of hot water and stir until lovely and smooth. Coat the tops of the éclairs in chocolate, then chill in the fridge.

5 Whip the cream and fill a piping bag with a star nozzle. Hull and slice the strawberries.

6 Slice the éclairs open lengthways. Do not cut all the way through, leave one side intact as a hinge.

7 Pipe the cream into each éclair and decorate with sliced strawberries.

***

Crêpes Normandes

The first time I ordered cooking apples for 'Le Moulin de Mule' in Rouen there was a pause at the end of the phone. Which type of apple did I want... Belle de Boskoff, Reinette, Belchard. There are 600 varieties of apple in Normandy, and a mentality associating Bramleys as the unique cooking apple was not going to suffice. For sweet apples, you are unlikely to taste anything better than the great big beauties from Brambletye biodynamic farm at Forest Row. Seek out their stall at the Friday Lewes farmers' market.

Ingredients: 8 portions
For the crêpes:
120 gm Doves Farm flour, light wholemeal
120 gm plain white flour
2 eggs
500 ml semi-skimmed milk
100 ml sunflower oil

For the filling and sauce:
600 gm Brambletye sweet apples
600 gm cooking apples
Ground cinnamon
100 gm raisins
200 ml apple juice
150 ml honey
2 punnets of raspberries

Method:

1 Beat the eggs into the flour, and gradually incorporate the milk. To avoid a lumpy batter, beat hard until all the flour is combined into a smooth paste. Thereafter it is an easier job to combine the remaining milk. Rest in the fridge for an hour.

2 Peel the cooking apples. Quarter all the apples, remove the core and slice thinly. Place in a pan with a little apple juice, raisins and a generous amount of cinnamon. Cover and stew over a low flame. Stir in the honey and leave to cook until the fruit has softened Add more sweetness and spice if necessary, turn out into a bowl and set aside.

3 Tip the berries into a pan with a little apple juice and honey. Stew till soft, liquidise and pour into a sauce boat.

4 Place a brush in a little jug of oil. Anoint the pan with oil, and when almost smoking, swirl a small ladle of crêpe batter around the pan. Return the pan to the heat and after 30 seconds, bang the pan on the stove. Edge around the sides with a palette knife, and flip the pancake over.

5 When both sides are done, turn out onto a plate. You can pile successive pancakes on top of each other.

6 This dish can be warmed in the oven or served cold. Spoon some apple mixture into each crêpe and roll into a cigar. Coat with raspberry coulis. For absolute decadence serve with a scoop of Downsview honeycomb ice cream.

***

Orange & Honey Clafoutis

Clafoutis is a fruity French Yorkshire pudding that makes a simple and original dessert. Bees have been having a hard time lately, diminished by neoncotinoid insecticides. Fortunately, excellent products still survive on either side of the Channel. At Normandy markets, look out for a wonderful range of honeys produced by the apiculture Marc Fourneau. Paynes Farm is the main Sussex supplier, and distinctive honeys emerge from unexpected sources like Moulescoomb and Portslade. Recently I discovered a delicious dark Shoreham honey in the deli on the High Street. It was supplied by Luciano Scandian who also has hives in Steyning and Worthing. Luciano prefers not to adulterate honey by cooking, content with a dollop on porridge or yoghurt. Perhaps this recipe will tempt him to spin a little honey on a caramelised Yorkshire pudding.

Ingredients: 8 portions

    120 gm Doves Farm light wholemeal flour
    120 gm soft white flour
    2 eggs
    400 ml semi-skimmed milk
    200 ml sunflower oil
    2 large oranges
    200 ml clear honey

Method:

1 Using a peeler, or a canelle knife, remove the orange zest in strips, taking care to leave the pith behind. Blanch in boiling water for 20 seconds, drain and chop very finely.

2 With a sharp knife, remove the layer of pith to leave the juicy orange, cut out the segments and set aside. Squeeze the juice from the remaining pulp and use as part of the batter liquid.

3 Make the Yorkshire pudding batter, following the directions in the crêpe recipe. Use the squeezed orange juice as part of the recipe liquid, and stir in the chopped orange zest. The finished batter should be slightly thicker than for crêpes. Leave to rest for an hour.

4 Set the oven to 200°c, gas mark 6. Coat the base of 8 Yorkshire tins with oil and heat in the oven till almost smoking. Pour in the batter and cook till well risen but still soft – about 20 minutes. Place 3 orange segments on each pud, and spin the honey all over. Return to the oven till crisp and caramelised.

***

Summer Pudding

Summer pudding is that rare thing, a totally healthy dessert. The fruit provides loads of fibre and antioxidant vitamins, and there is no need to add any sugar. Roundstone Farm at Ferring offers every variety of berry and currant as well as their own rhubarb. 'Sewards Strawberries' is close to Bolney Wine Estate, offering an opportunity to kick off your sandals, lay in the grass and indulge in strawberries and bubbly.

Ingredients: 6 portions

1 thick cut malted granary loaf
1 large punnet strawberries
1 large punnet blackberries
Any other fresh berries or currants that come to hand
150 ml apple juice
2 large dessert spoons of clear honey

Method:

1 A granary loaf lends taste and texture to the dish. Spread out the slices to absorb the dryness of a summer's day. A few hours in the sun makes the bread easier to cut.

2 Hull the strawberries and put all the fruit in a saucepan with a little apple juice. Heat gently under cover and stir in the honey. When the fruit has softened and started to simmer, pour into colander resting in a larger bowl. Do not be tempted to cook the fruit longer, as it will turn almost totally into juice. Set aside the fruit to cool.

3 Cut the bread slices into 1 inch thick 'soldiers' and line the sides of a pudding basin. Create whatever shapes are needed to make a close fit. Cut out two semicircles to fit the base.

4 Take the pieces of bread one at a time, dip in the berry juice and line the pudding basin with the dry side facing inwards. Do the same with the semicircles and then turn the fruit into the bread lining. Spoon in some berry juice so that the whole pudding is moist without being saturated.

5 Cut out 2–3 shapes of bread to form a lid, dip both sides in juice and lay on top of the fruit. Trim off any of the 'soldiers' that might be sticking up above the lid.

Cover with clingfilm, and lay a saucer or small plate that fits on top. Place a weight on the plate and leave to rest in the fridge overnight. The pectin in the fruit acts as a setting agent.

6 Turn out the pudding and serve with remaining berry juice and a dollop of good yoghurt.

***

Sussex Plum Pudding

Sussex kitchens were once famous for puddings. The most distinctive was 'Sussex Pond Pudding', where an entire lemon was wrapped inside a suet paste. Suet has an extremely high saturated fat content, so this recipe does without. Many plum pudding recipes were made with dried fruit like currants and raisins, but this one uses fresh plums.

Ingredients: 6–8 servings

For the sponge:
200 gm butter
120 gm caster sugar
4 eggs
400 gm self raising flour
Juice and zest of a lemon

For the stewed plums:
1 kilo red plums
200 ml apple juice
2–3 dessert spoons clear honey

Method:

1 Grease the pudding basin with a little butter.

2 Stew the plums gently under cover in the apple juice and honey. When softened, spoon out some plums to line the bottom of the pudding basin. Blend the remainder and pour into a sauce boat.

3 Cream together the butter and sugar. Gradually beat in the eggs, one at a time. Finally combine the lemon juice, zest and the flour. Turn the sponge mix into the pudding basin so it is two thirds full.

4 Use string to secure a pleated greaseproof lid on top of the pudding basin. The pleats will allow the sponge to rise. Steam for about 90 minutes. In the absence of a steamer, set the oven to a moderate heat and place the pudding basin in a deep dish filled with warm water.

5 Turn out the pudding and serve with plum sauce.

***

Simnel cake
'Cocoa Loco'

Sarah and Rory Payne run a small family business producing 'joy confections' from organic ingredients. They involve talented cooks 'who dabble in bold flavours and dreamy textures.' Just a taste of the enthusiasm which radiates from their website. Here is an Easter treat.

www.cocoaloco.co.uk

Ingredients: 15 cakes

175g melted butter
225g self raising flour
1 tsp cinnamon
1 tsp mixed spice
100g muscovado sugar
100g mixed dried fruit
100g dried apricots chopped

100g Cocoa Loco dark chocolate grated
3 eggs
150 ml milk
350 gm marzipan
200 gm apricot jam for glaze
15 chocolate mini eggs

Method:

1 Preheat your oven to 180°C gas mark 4. Grease and line a 17x27cm rectangular tin cook the apricot jam with a little water to make a glaze.

2 Mix all dry ingredients: flour, cinnamon, muscovado sugar, mixed fruit and dried apricots. Grate the chocolate and 100g marzipan and add to the dry ingredients.

3 Whisk the eggs and add milk, then pour onto the dry mixture with the melted butter and stir together with a large spoon.

4 Pour the mixture into the tin. Bake for 30 minutes until well risen and firm. Leave cake to cool. Cut cake into 15 squares.

5 Roll out marzipan then using a flower shaped cutter, cut out 15 shapes. Place a marzipan flower on top of each cake, using the apricot jam to stick the flower in place. Finish with a chocolate egg on top.

***

Moose's Fruity Flapjack
Red Roaster Coffee House

What better way to end a meal than with an excellent cup of coffee? 'The Red Roaster' café in St. James Street reflects the colour and vibrancy of Brighton life. Big bold exhibitions decorate the walls, hanging wood sculptures fill the vaulted ceiling and at night the floor is swept by tango dancers. A magnificent roaster stands gleaming behind the counter, presided over by resident coffee expert Paul Stephens. Akin to a master vintner, Paul can describe the aroma and origin of a coffee bean at one hundred paces. The café offers a good line in homemade snacks, and Moose who makes the flapjacks suggests using rolled oats to improve the texture. Red Roaster also provides coffee beans for the 'Espresso' beer produced by Dark Star, a small brewery based at Partridge Green.

www.redroaster.co.uk

Ingredients: 6 portions

150g butter (or margarine for vegans)
80g soft brown sugar
150g golden syrup
250g organic rolled oats from Infinity Foods
140g dried cranberries or apricots

Method:

1 Preheat the oven to 180°c, gas mark 4. Lightly grease a small square cornered baking tin.

2 Blend the butter, sugar and syrup together in a pan over medium heat. Add the oats, then the cranberries or apricots (or any other dried fruit of your choice). Stir well.

3 Spoon the mixture into the tin, pressing well into the corners and making the surface even. Place in the middle of the oven for 15–20 minutes, until golden-brown and gently bubbling.

4 Remove from the oven and allow to cool before cutting.

***

Chapter 6

Getting there by Bike

If your concept of leisure does not involve relentless exertion, then bike and train provides the perfect solution. This little chapter explores three cycle routes which follow disused railway lines.

The 'Cuckoo Trail' takes you from Polegate to Heathfield, and apart from a brief flirtation with roads at Hailsham, is completely car-free. Get out at Polegate station, turn right along the High Street, right at the roundabout and you have arrived.

An ancient rite of alliteration deems that all the encampments along the Cuckoo Trail begin with the letter 'H'. Hidden Spring vineyard near Horam has home grown wine and cider. Hellingly has Blackstock Open Farm with big-eyed llamas you will want to adopt and take home. Hailsham has tinkling teashops, and every August Bank Holiday Heathfield hosts 'Le Marché', a bonanza of French food and drink.

Michelam Priory is signposted along the way and well worth the visit, the entrance equipped with penny-farthing bike stands to lasso your trusty stead. From there it's a pleasant ride to Berwick, where you can reconnect with the train line.

The 'Downs Link Route 222' follows the redundant rail line from Shoreham to Guildford. Make for Rope Tackle at the end of Shoreham High Street, turn right at the roundabout, and after passing under the railway bridge, the cycle path follows the River Adur. There is a goodly supply of real ale en route, Badger beer on the riverbank at Bramber, and the Dark Star brewery at Partridge Green. From Christ's Hospital you could be brave and carry on to Guildford. Alternatively, take the train to Arundel and enjoy the Wetlands Centre that lies in the river valley. The coastal service back to Brighton runs from Ford.

Cycling is a joy in Upper Normandy, with little 'D' roads unspoiled by traffic. The simplest route to take after arriving at Dieppe, is West along the coast to Fécamp and Etretat, a roller coaster ride between cliff tops and beaches. Cycle to the end of the pedestrianised Grande Rue, cross the road at the lights and climb the steep hill signed for the castle. The coastal road is the D75.

The railway south to Rouen follows the little River Scie and passes through attractive villages at Longueville, Auffay and Clères. You can do the whole 40 kilometers by bike, or hop on the train half way. The D153 leads to the D3 which takes you all the way to the centre of Rouen.

Having arrived in the capital of Normandy, there is a lovely route following the Seine as it winds its' way West to the tumbledown Abbey at Jumièges and the Roman amphitheatre at Lillebonne. Follow the banks of the Rive

Droite to Croisset Canteleu, then take the lovely new cycle path to Sahurs. Jump on the little red ferry that takes you for free to La Bouille.

'L'Avenue Verte' is a famous cycle route, eventually destined to link Paris with London. It follows a disused railway track, undulating through the pastoral landscape of Le Pays du Bray. Finding the beginning can be tricky as sign posting is elusive. Turn sharp right outside the ferry terminal at Dieppe, then left at the iron bridge and immediately right. You are now on the road to Arques-la-Bataille, from where 'L'Avenue Verte' continues to Neufchatel and Forges-les-Eaux. If you are happy to wander, the Avenue passes close to many of the artisan food producers recommended earlier in the book. For example, the village of Bellencombre has a lovely goat cheese farm and a tiny cider museum.

You will find 10 maps with cycle routes in *A Mule in Rouen – a Discovery of Upper Normandy*.

Sydney Street Bikes in Brighton often arrange trips across to France. Tel: 01273 624700/747222.

'Bricycles' is an excellent campaigning group which also organises forays into Viking territory. www.bricycles.org.uk

Bon voyage à vélo!

The Cuckoo Trail

Dieppe

Royal Pavilion Gardens

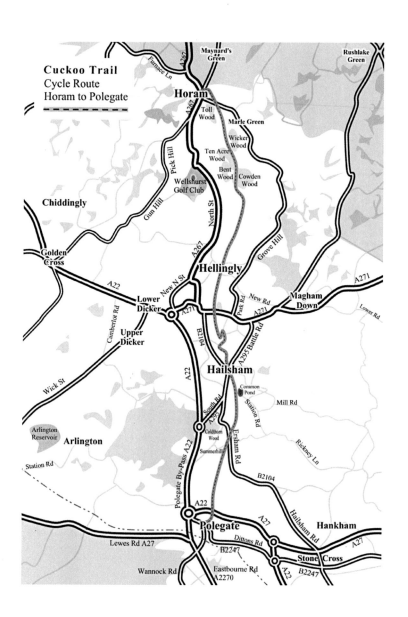